SPIES AND STARS

ALSO BY CHARLOTTE BINGHAM

Non-fiction
Coronet Among the Weeds
Coronet Among the Grass
MI5 and Me: A Coronet Among the
Spooks

Novels
Lucinda
The Business
In Sunshine or in Shadow
Stardust
Nanny
Change of Heart
Grand Affair
Love Song
The Kissing Garden
Country Wedding
The Blue Note
The Love Knot
Summertime
Distant Music
The Magic Hour
Friday's Girl
Out of the Blue
In Distant Fields
The White Marriage
Goodnight Sweetheart
The Enchanted
The Land of Summer
The Daisy Club

Love Quartet
Belgravia
Country Life
At Home
By Invitation

Nightingale Saga
To Hear a Nightingale
The Nightingale Sings

Debutantes Saga
Debutantes
The Season

The Bexham Trilogy
The Chestnut Tree
The Wind Off the Sea
The Moon at Midnight

Eden Saga
Daughters of Eden
The House of Flowers

Mums on the Run Series
Mums on the Run
A Dip Before Breakfast

WITH TERENCE BRADY
Victoria Series
Victoria
Victoria and Company

Honestly Series
No, Honestly
Yes, Honestly

Upstairs, Downstairs Series
Rose's Story

SPIES AND STARS

MI5, Showbusiness and Me

Charlotte Bingham

BLOOMSBURY PUBLISHING
LONDON · OXFORD · NEW YORK · NEW DELHI · SYDNEY

BLOOMSBURY PUBLISHING
Bloomsbury Publishing Plc
50 Bedford Square, London, WC1B 3DP, UK

BLOOMSBURY, BLOOMSBURY PUBLISHING and the Diana logo are
trademarks of Bloomsbury Publishing Plc

First published in Great Britain 2019

A catalogue record for this book is available from the British Library

Library of Congress Cataloguing-in-Publication data has been applied for

ISBN: HB: 978-1-5266-0868-0; TPB: 978-1-5266-0881-9; EBOOK: 978-1-5266-0879-6

2 4 6 8 10 9 7 5 3 1

Typeset by Integra Software Services Pvt. Ltd.

Printed and bound in Great Britain by CPI Group (UK) Ltd, Croydon CR0 4YY

To find out more about our authors and books visit www.bloomsbury.com and
sign up for our newsletters

For Terence, in memory of all the gaiety and the laughter — but most of all the fun!

'Let other pens dwell on guilt and misery. I quit such odious subjects as soon as I can, impatient to restore everybody not greatly in fault themselves to tolerable comfort, and to have done with all the rest.'

Jane Austen, *Mansfield Park*

*The action of this book takes place in
England in the 1950s.*

UNDERCOVER

It seems to me now that Harry did rather well working as an undercover agent for my father, although at the time it was not what you could call a slam dunk.

Harry had already had the misfortune to fall in love with me. On top of this calamity, and even more unfortunately for him, I came with a Top Secret file attached to my suitcase on account of my father being very active as an MI5 officer. The one thing that Harry had going for him was that he was an actor. Now this may seem unlikely, and I can see that it might, but my father was pursuing a popular theme with British security folk at the time, namely that our airwaves and films were being infiltrated by communist-leaning people who were intent on bending minds and hearts towards Stalin and the Iron Curtain. According to the secret service's thinking, pretty soon the whole population would be pleading to work on collective farms and singing 'The Red Flag' in tavern and cottage, not to mention pub and club.

I have to say I did not see it that way, and I told my father as much, which did not go down terribly well, as it wouldn't. In fact, he was so unconvinced that he walked off into the garden smoking a cigarette while wearing the kind of expression I imagined he used when interrogating a double agent.

My thought was that, first of all, the British people liked nothing better than a laugh and there were not many of those to be had with communists. Also that the goodly British people would be much more likely to opt for Flanagan and Allen singing 'Show Me The Way to Go Home' than 'The Red Flag'; and as for country pursuits, they would never swap listening to *The Archers*, the popular radio serial about farming life in Britain, for one about collective farming. I maintained that people would take to the streets if the BBC took this staple of our national life off our airwaves. Of course, I couldn't leave it at that, could I? Even after Father's ominous exit from the drawing room and the smell of cigarette smoke beginning to permeate his beloved garden, I did not climb down from my soap box but went on speaking to a room devoid of everyone except my mother and me.

'You've really annoyed your father now, Lottie,' she said in a *'thank you very much for that'* voice.

I nodded. I knew I had but I could not shut up. It was one of my worst faults. I knew this because my girlfriend Arabella told me as much every time we had a coffee together, and Harry said the same, so they must both have been right, but that didn't stop me. Mrs Graham, who helped us with cooking and dusting things, on a daily basis, always agreed with the general verdict.

'You will have your say no matter what, Miss Lottie,' she had intoned to me since I was tall enough to steal her jam tarts from the sideboard. 'And one of these days it will get you up to your neck in scalding water.'

I left for the nearby coffee bar and the company of Harry, which although not always comfortable, I mean the coffee bar – oh, and Harry too on a bad day – was at least lively. Better that than the awful silence that had fallen over Dingley Dell, as our house in leafy Kensington has always been known to its fans. As I walked to meet him I could only hope that Melville and Hal, the two actors who lodged with us, would be back soon to divert my mother, as they always did, with talk of tatty theatrical tours and perfidious producers.

This particular early-summer evening Harry was looking very Hamlet, which was only natural since he was out of work – as Hamlet must have been, because let's face it, the poor fellow was fairly unemployable. All that business about seeing his father's ghost – and that's before he starts on at Ophelia about becoming a nun – I mean, talk about beastly. He could at least have wished her better luck with someone nicer than himself. I tell you, Hamlet might have been a prince but he was certainly no gentleman.

'Still no calls or offers?' I asked tactlessly as I sat down opposite Harry. I had started to consider myself fairly well versed in dealing with actors.

I had discovered from Hal and Melville that the best way to cope with an actor's depression was to get on with it: grasp the nettle. Hal and Melville, by the way, while pursuing their stage and screen careers were also in the way of reporting back to my father on the extreme left-wing activities of their fellow thespians.

Harry looked away at the traffic moving slowly past the window of the coffee bar. 'I am thinking of leaving Gus,' he finally announced, in the tone of someone who has just discovered they have chickenpox.

Gus was Harry's current actor's agent. Harry had gone through quite a few agents.

'Might be a good thing,' I offered, while at the same time wondering who else was left who would take Harry on. His list of credits was about as long as my attention span.

Harry sighed, deeply. It was the kind of sigh that might easily be heard over the radio waves when a tractor had broken down on *The Archers* and there were no spare parts to be had even for ready money.

'I like Gus,' Harry continued. 'But he will keep nicking from me when we play squash.'

'He really should wait to nick from you until after he's got you a job,' I reasoned. 'There would be more to nick.'

'Exactly. If he's like this when I'm out of work, what is he going to be like when I'm a star?'

I looked away. Harry's stardom was a bit of a way off just at the moment. I knew this from Hal and Melville, the actors already mentioned who also happened to be undercover agents for my father. They were very different characters, but their verdict on acting was ominously unanimous.

'Do not become an actor unless you would commit suicide doing anything else,' Hal had boomed at Harry.

'And it does not help to be a married man,' Melville warned him. 'If you want to be a star, you must remain single. It is just a fact.'

'Dear boy, if you stay an actor, you will always be miserable,' Hal had added happily.

'So why are you two actors?' I asked them when Harry had left, wearing the expression of one about to take an overdose. I had not followed him as I was determined to get to the bottom of why they should both have willingly turned their backs on marriage and a happy life.

Melville and Hal looked at each other and then shrugged their shoulders.

'Didn't know any better, darling!' Hal boomed.

There was no doubt that Harry had been cast down by them, but not quite enough to believe them, and now he was sitting in the coffee bar, and determined on leaving his agent, he was actually looking more cheerful.

There is no point in deterring someone who is on course to do something, but I knew that once Harry left me and went back to the bachelor flat he shared with several other actors, he would probably find it more difficult to leave his agent than he thought, even if Gus was in the habit of taking Harry's small change when he was in the shower at the squash club.

Next time we met, same coffee bar, same time, Harry was looking thoughtful once more.

'I am still thinking of leaving Gus, but not until he has got me a job. Dermot thinks I should wait until then, and I agree with him.'

Dermot shared a bedroom with Harry, which worked quite well because they were polar opposites. Dermot's half of the room was a hard-hat area.

Happily, the bed was always covered by a heap of old copies of the *Daily Mirror* and full ashtrays, not to mention library books that hadn't been returned since Hitler invaded Poland. This meant that no one could see the greying sheets and prison-service blankets. Harry's side, on the other hand, was always up for Matron's first prize – bed made with hospital corners, everything spick and span.

'Dermot is absolutely right; you should stay with Gus, just for the moment,' I agreed, while immediately losing interest.

'I am up to go for an audition next week, a part in a revue called *Fools Rush In.*'

'Oh good,' I said, but being a theatre snob found myself wishing that it was an audition for the Fool in *King Lear*, not just playing the fool in a revue. 'Hal's going to Broadway with *Lear* and Melville's opening with Beatrice La Motte in *Birdie Bye Bye.*'

'Beatrice La Motte is far too old for Birdie!'

'I know,' I agreed without knowing much about it, which is another habit of mine. 'But Melville says it is work, and at least he will be *seen.*'

'Dermot says work is thin on the ground for every-one, that theatre has not recovered from people like Laurence Olivier putting on verse plays, and now idiots like Dermot are going around saying that the well-made play has had it.'

'That's a bit rich from someone who can't even make his own bed.'

'The *Manchester Guardian* may be starting a campaign against the proscenium arch.'

'They have to do something with summer coming on,' I said, waving to a waitress who was doing nothing. 'Two more coffees, please.'

'No – just one, thank you.'

Harry looked embarrassed.

I stared at him. Very well, coffee was ninepence more here than in other coffee bars, but the seats were plush and there was a good view of the High Street.

Then the penny dropped. Harry was actually skint, which was why he was suddenly only a one-coffee man.

I put my hand over his, which we both knew was big coming from me, because showing emotion is not my strongest point.

'I'm flush,' I murmured.

'You look fine to me,' he joked, then to the waitress, 'Two coffees, please.'

'Anyone would think you had sold a book or something,' he went on, referring to my long lonely evenings at Dingley Dell trying to write a novel so as to earn some extra money while keeping on my secretarial work. 'I don't know how you stand being a secretary at that War Office place.'

'And I don't know how you stand being out of work.'

'Here's to Lady Luck, Lottie,' he said fervently.

We raised our coffee cups to each other, and spent the rest of the evening in a very pleasant way that happily needs no expenditure, and certainly no description.

The following week my mother's expression was grim again. I knew why because Mrs Graham had told me.

'Your mother's not happy with you going out with the same man all the time, Miss Lottie. She thinks you should broaden your horizons. That just going out with one actor is bad for you.'

'I don't think I have the energy to go out with a whole company of them,' I replied, laughing.

Mrs Graham did not join in.

'She thinks you could do better for yourself.'

Actually I agreed with this. It was obvious that I could do better than Harry, and to give him his due Harry could do much better than me. But for the moment we were stuck with each other and I could only go to work at the War Office as a secretary to Commander Steerforth, and cross my fingers that Harry would get a part in the revue, which he didn't.

'Who *did* get it?' I asked.

Harry looked away, and then back at me. There was a long pause. 'You'll never guess.'

'Try me.'

Harry cleared his throat. 'Dermot.'

'*What?*'

'Yes, it turned out he heard me talking to Gus about it at the flat, and immediately rang his agent. Actually, Tony and Dermot both did, and they both went up for it and Dermot got it. And he can't even sing, really.'

'Teach you to keep your trap shut, Harry.'

'Too right, Lottie-bags. I mean to say, though – I never thought – I mean we are meant to be *friends*.'

'Melville always says there are no such things as friends when it comes to agents, auditions, or the bar bill.'

'Did he find that in a Christmas cracker?' Harry shook his head. 'I keep telling myself the revue is sure to be a flop, and serve Dermot right.'

'Exactly. It might not even come to the West End,' I said in an attempt to comfort him.

'Last time he borrows my milk or butter.'

Harry brightened at the idea of putting his meagre rations off limits. 'But the good news is,' he went on, 'I'm up for a part in a film, playing a young German officer. It's a war story.'

'I didn't think it was a Doris Day musical,' I replied, frowning.

Actually I was frowning because the mention of German rang bells. I could suddenly see an opportunity for Harry and myself to curry favour with my father. I was still in his bad books for saying that people would always choose washing machines and a telly over communism so why did we need to stay so vigilant against it?

'I can't speak German,' Harry went on happily. 'But I can do the accent all right. *Ya kohl* and *main Herr!* And that sort of thing. I've been practising already.'

'Wait! I have had a thought.'

'Please, don't have a thought, Lottie; you know what happened last time.'

'My father speaks German like a native. It's practically his first language. He speaks it so well, I'll ask him to help you.'

Instantly Harry stopped looking cheerful. He had not darkened the doors of Dingley Dell since my father had discovered him climbing in at the basement window. Worse than that, and for reasons I will not bore you with, my father had been carrying a swordstick at the time – MI5 officers carry funny things – and it fell apart at Harry's feet, which turned him into a jelly on a plate.

'I don't think you should bother your father, really I don't, Lottie. I mean with all that he has on – fighting communism tooth and nail, and matters of extreme state and so forth and so fifth – I wouldn't dream of bothering him.'

'No, honestly, he can help you with your accent. Make sure you sound as if you live in a mountain chateau as German officers are meant to do.' I paused, and then by way of comforting Harry, said, 'He can be nice sometimes, really he can.'

'I'd rather not, Lottie.'

But it was too late and Harry knew it. I had seen an opening to break the awful silence that had fallen between my father and me. Besides, once I had an idea it had to become something more.

A few days later, it *had* become something more, a Sunday morning appointment for Harry.

I had arranged it for Sunday morning because it was a favourite time of the week for my father, what with Melville at the drawing-room piano playing his show numbers and Mrs Graham in the kitchen cooking roast beef and Yorkshire pudding, the comforting smells wafting up from the basement.

'He's sure to want to get a few in before going in to lunch, so he won't be long with you, I wouldn't have thought,' I assured Harry.

'I don't think this is a very good idea, Lottie, really I don't.'

'You can't back out now. No one backs out on my father once he says he'll see them.'

Harry thought for a minute.

'I don't suppose they do.' He shuddered. 'Might end up in a sack at the bottom of the Thames.'

'Or they might swap you for a double agent and send you to Siberia. That happens,' I said, gleefully.

Harry looked so dejected I ordered him another coffee.

When Sunday morning dawned it was a lovely day. And sure enough Melville started to play some of my father's favourite numbers from the old musicals, and what with the smell of roast beef cooking and the sound of the piano playing, I thought Harry would have a good chance with the German speaking, and my father who dearly loved to be of help would put me back in his good books.

I will say this for Harry: he managed to climb up the steps to the front doors of Dingley Dell and walk inside to knock on my father's study door without passing out. I had already joked that I would stand by with a wet towel and some smelling salts but when I saw Harry's pallor I realised it was not such a joke after all.

I left him going into the study and fled to the drawing room where I pretended not to have a care in the world, until my mother came to the door and beckoned to me.

Outside in the hall, she pointed to the study.

'Your father is in there making a quite beastly row.'

I stood outside the door with her and listened. It was true. There was a beastly row.

'I think they're singing,' I said, after a bit.

'Your father is only allowed to sing when Melville's playing,' my mother stated. 'If he must sing on his own he has to do it in the garden, or on the pavement outside. He knows that.'

'I think he's trying to be helpful.'

'The last time your father was helpful we had to call an ambulance.' She sighed, which made me think she had been listening to *The Archers* too much. 'I had better go in and do something about all this before it gets out of hand.'

Things getting out of hand was something that my mother dreaded even more than the Bomb. They loomed large in her life. I increasingly saw her as a martyr to the nation's security, what with the constant dinner parties she was forced to give at Dingley Dell to keep my father's agents happy at all times, and the likelihood of swordsticks falling apart – it was a hard life for her.

As the daughter of an MI5 officer and not just a theatre snob, but a car snob too, I could only regret that my father had to go about in such unremarkable cars, and very often in a very dubious-looking Mackintosh. These are sacrifices that the nation as a whole cannot appreciate, but to the family of a man running undercover agents, they are very real. In the course of his work my father had to affect many different disguises. One of them he had described to me. 'Man Leaning on Bar in Mac with Pipe' was good cover while listening, and in this character he picked up goodness knows how much information.

'You would be surprised,' he said, 'how much people will confide to a stranger after a pint or two, especially if he listens to them. Not many people are good at listening, you know.'

The truth was that my father would have loved a large Bentley and a gold wristwatch, not to mention a cashmere coat, but it would have made him stand out in the places where he went to gather information. His great-est regret was not being able to get into the army on account of poor eyesight, so he'd elected to fight for his country another way, by doing covert security work in defence of the nation. As a terminally modest man, it suited him fine.

Not that any of this was on my mind when I pushed open his study door that morning.

The scene upon which I stumbled was extraordinary to me: my father, arm-in-arm with Harry of all people, marching up and down his study – rug rolled back – while at the same time singing what I imagined from the military sound of it must be a German marching song. But then Germans speaking German have a habit of sounding cross, even if they're being nice and kind.

Harry had the unfortunate air of a man being marched off to the police station.

'March, young man, march!'

Harry marched and marched again. Sweat started to bead on his forehead before my father finally stopped, perhaps remembering it was Sunday and time to go to the drinks cupboard. He shook Harry's hand and walked off.

On the way back to his flat Harry was speechless, and with due deference to his artistic ordeal, I did not break the silence. He spoke at last as he put his key in the front door.

'If I don't get this job on the film it will not be your father's fault,' he said in a sober voice. 'He is a very forceful man.'

'But why were you singing?' I asked as we walked into the dark hall of the flat that always smelled of the kind of cooking you are very glad you are not being asked to eat. I went on, 'My father can't sing in tune, which is why he loves to hear Melville singing and playing. It is why he loves musicals. They are wonderful to him.'

'Your father maintains that the best way to learn a language is first to sing in it. He said schools should do this, it makes learning more fun.'

I nodded vaguely, my mind already on whether or not Harry would get the job.

As a matter of fact, I thought of nothing else for the next few days. I so hoped that he would get the job. It would make such a difference to him.

Time went by, as it tends to do, at a very boring and slow pace, day after day after day – and still no news. My mother knew that I was worried because I kept going to the kitchen to polish my shoes, which was so out of character that she bought me a health tonic.

And still Harry heard nothing, and still my shoes were so highly polished they could have gone on parade at Trooping the Colour for the Queen's official birthday.

One day I woke up determined not to think about it any longer. And I didn't think about it. I went to meet Harry at the coffee bar still in determined mood.

He was already there. I sat down opposite him. The moment I saw the look in his eyes I knew that I would be paying for coffee for the next week.

'Gus rang.'

'At last.'

'Yup. He even managed to remember my number, which is big for Gus.'

'And?'

I knew not to sound too interested so I made sure to say 'and' at the same time as I was beckoning to the waitress.

'And I did not get the part.'

I sighed, very heavily,

'Oh, sugar, what a drying shame. After all your work.'

'I know—'

'Well, why didn't you? You polished up your German no end.'

'I know, and they said my accent was perfect, but—'

'But?'

'Apparently, the director told Gus, I kept sounding as if I was singing it.'

So it was coffee on me – oh, and cake – for the next week.

THE INVITATION

Arabella and I first became friends at the War Office. In some ways it was unavoidable since we sat opposite each other tapping away at our ancient Underwood typewriters. Happily, a bit like Dermot and Harry in their shared room at the flat, Arabella and I were complete opposites. To begin with she was very beautiful, and I was not. This was not false modesty on my part. Not even Mrs Graham, who quite liked me, had ever been able to say more of my looks than 'you'll do'.

Then there was the question of our temperaments. Arabella was organised and considered. When faced with a crisis of any kind, she pulled back and assumed a sphinx-like expression that always boded well because it meant she was thinking, which was not something I did unless I was on a bus, and then only if no one was sitting next to me.

At this particular moment in time Arabella was looking even more sphinx-like than usual. I had told her something — well, confessed would be a better word —

and it had sent her into a mentally crossed-leg position accompanied by the dream-like trance that gave her eyes the look of someone seeing far into the future.

'I don't think that is a very good idea,' she announced, at last.

I could not but agree with her.

'Whose idea was it, exactly?'

I know I was looking uneasy. I must have been, because Arabella abandoned her trance-like state and offered me a Polo mint.

'It was Melville's idea,' I said, taking one. 'He put it up to my father. He likes Harry and doesn't want to see him starve. Being an actor is eighty per cent starvation, Melville says, and he thought it might help Harry to have a bit of money. At the moment he only eats cornflakes for lunch and a Marmite sandwich for supper. The other day his tummy rumbled so much when we were in the coffee bar the manager called the plumber.'

Arabella flared her nostrils lightly, which was one of her more endearing habits when she was thinking hard.

'I can see what Melville means about trying to create some sort of income, but he surely doesn't know Harry too well?'

'No, he doesn't know Harry very well at all,' I agreed. 'Melville has tried to put him off acting, but that would be like trying to put me off coffee.'

'I wouldn't have thought he did know Harry – even suggesting such a thing. But the thought of Harry working undercover is terrifying. He finds life in the open difficult enough.'

I had to agree with Arabella. What on earth would Harry be like coping with aliases and passwords – and, worst of all for Harry, not being able to tell anyone what he was up to? Because keeping his trap shut was not something Harry had ever done, at least not in front of me.

'Probably nothing will come of it,' Arabella said in a kindly tone, which we both knew meant that she hoped to goodness it wouldn't.

Unfortunately, I knew that something had already come of Melville's suggestion. My father had called me into his study and announced that he wanted Harry's address. I would have given anything to tell him the wrong one, but I was not that brave. If your father was an MI5 officer you had to be a complete duffer not to realise that treading the straight and narrow was a better choice than being sent on an exchange visit with a Russian agent. So I watched my father with a sinking heart as he wrote down Harry's address very carefully. Following this he told me he would write Harry a letter, which I knew would begin: 'If you care to come to the Cleveland Hotel on a date of your choosing I may be able to help you with something of interest regarding your future.'

I knew this was how MI5 letters always began, because my father had told me that this was the kind of letter he had received before the war, when he was invited to join MI5 instead of climbing into a uniform. Now he sealed the envelope and gave me the letter to post to Harry. As I was walking to the post I found myself tempted to throw it in a bin, but once again I did not dare, for the very good reason that the non-arrival of Harry's letter would have placed me under suspicion, which in turn could lead to that dread of all dreads – an interrogation.

So I posted the letter and waited for the inevitable repercussion, which happened in only a very short space of time.

Harry arrived white-faced at the coffee bar, and since he was carrying the letter it was obvious that it was not because we had changed our daily meeting place to somewhere cheaper.

'Was this your idea?' he demanded, looking fraught. 'And why would your father want me to have lunch with him? He says he has "something of interest to impart to me".'

I shook my head. My head-shaking implied it was nothing to do with me, which it truly was not.

'Whose idea was it then?'

I knew you must never betray your sources, so I went on shrugging my shoulders and looking dumb, which was not difficult for me. Quite apart from anything else, I knew that Melville would get into Harry's bad books for life if I told him the suggestion had come from him, however well intended.

'Your father wants me to meet him for lunch at the Cleveland.'

'Well, that's nice. The food is so good there.'

'I can't meet him for lunch at the Cleveland — my only suit is at the cleaner's.'

'In that case, just write back and thank him and say you will have to wait for Sketchley's to send your suit back. He will quite understand.'

Harry looked close to suicide.

'Why does he want me to go to lunch with him? I mean why? I am only a two-bit actor, what possible interest could I be to him?'

I tried to look vague and innocent, and after failing horribly I sipped my coffee and wished we were back in the more expensive coffee bar where there was a view of the High Street, which was always such a nice distraction when things got awkward.

'What can he want with me?'

I looked at Harry. He had the air of someone who had just seen something worse than terrible; he had seen something incredibly embarrassing. I sometimes thought that embarrassment was actually one of the worst sorts of tortures. I mean, who would not rather break their arm than be laughed at because their skirt was caught up in their shopping?

'Maybe he just wants to give you a good lunch because he knows you're having trouble getting work?'

Harry shook his head.

'If that were the case he would have asked me round to Dingley Dell.'

'You don't have to go.'

'I do. You know I do. I have to go.'

Harry brightened suddenly.

'Maybe Sketchley's will lose my suit?'

The day of the lunch it was quite obvious that Sketchley's had not lost his suit. In fact, Harry looked very smart, and I said so in that rather irritating way that girlfriends do when they want to make someone feel better who is resigned to feeling terrible.

'You know where the Cleveland is?' Harry nodded. 'At least you will have a good meal; you could do with eating something other than cornflakes.'

Harry nodded again, speechless with fear. 'What's the best way to cope with your father?'

'I don't know really.' I thought for a second. 'Let him talk, perhaps?'

'He's not going to start singing again, is he?'

'No, no, he hardly ever sings, that was just a one-off to try to help you get a part.'

We were at the bus stop. Harry looked so frightened I gave him a quick hug, which made him have another thought just as the bus was arriving and he was hopping on to it.

'He's not going to make me marry you, is he?'

'Good heavens, no!' I called out, horrified. 'You're not what he calls suitable.'

There was just enough time for Harry to look relieved before the bus drove off and I turned to go back to the War Office.

'You're looking pasty,' Arabella observed, with some satisfaction.

'I'm feeling pasty,' I admitted miserably. 'Harry's having lunch at the Cleveland with my father.'

'Oh, crumbs,' Arabella said, winding a triplicate of A4 and carbon paper into her typewriter. 'That is a turn up for the worst.'

I agreed before going into Commander Steerforth's office to take dictation.

I was always cheered by Commander Steerforth. I had only to see him and I felt better. I thought it was something to do with his having been in the navy. This particular morning he was humming a little snatch of Gilbert and Sullivan, and as we both knew the words we were able to form a little duet with the bit that goes '*the Ruler of the Queen's Nav-ee*'.

As soon as that was over I whipped out my shorthand notebook and waited expectantly, pencil poised.

'You look pasty,' he said suddenly.

'I am feeling pasty,' I admitted.

'Anything you want to talk about?'

I looked at the dear, dear Commander and thought for a minute. I knew he was currently escorting Arabella's mother and they were having a nice time being decorous and going to theatres and operas and musicals and art galleries, and shopping at Harrods for very small things that could be carried home very easily. They were both single and enjoying life, and it suddenly seemed to me that it must be so nice to be single and middle-aged and enjoying life together after lots of other bits of life that had perhaps not been so enjoyable. 'I would not want to burden you with my problems, Commander Steerforth,' I told him.

'I should burden me if I were you,' he said happily. 'Once you've been in the navy you've heard everything, you know.'

'It's just that Harry – the man I am going out with at the moment … he's an out-of-work actor – is having lunch with my father today.'

Commander Steerforth rose to his feet and went to the window. There was a dreadful silence. Eventually he turned back and shook his head at me.

'No wonder you're looking pasty,' he said quietly. 'I wouldn't want to have lunch with your father, and I'm not an out-of-work actor.' He paused before going on. 'Your father is one of the most frightening men I have ever had to deal with.'

My boss looked across at me, his expression at its most serious.

'Why is he so frightening?' I asked, although I certainly would not disagree with this.

'The reason he is so frightening,' Commander Steerforth stated, after pausing to consider, 'is because he never, ever gets angry, and people who don't get angry are always feared. If you have noticed, when he is – shall we say – disquieted, he drops his voice, lower and lower and lower where most men raise theirs. Shouting is not something your father will ever have done.'

I nodded silently. It was true.

There was another long silence as Commander Steerforth left his position by the window and sank slowly down into his chair.

I waited before putting up a defence of my father and his frightening reputation.

'He can be very nice sometimes. I mean he tried to help Harry with his German accent for a film – it wasn't his fault it didn't have a very good outcome.'

'Oh, yes, he is the best pal in the world, I know that, but this poor chap, this Harry – I feel sorry for him.' The Commander shook his head, and then brightened suddenly. 'But perhaps something nice will come of the lunch, for once.'

I didn't like that 'for once'. And all the time I was taking dictation I thought of poor Harry on the bus, and then making his way into the Cleveland, and my father probably already at his table, waiting, because I knew he was always early for the good reason it put him at an advantage over people. Something else he had told me, but which I failed to practise myself because if I was early for someone they would just think I had got the time wrong.

I don't know what I thought would happen to Harry, but I certainly could not have imagined what did happen. The telephone on my desk rang. I knew it could not be Commander Steerforth because I had just seen him going off to meet Arabella's mother at the Royal Opera House. It was well past packing up time, which at the War Office was six o'clock, and I should have been flinging myself towards a 'vanishing nine' as the number nine buses were known to their regulars.

'Hallo?' I said, with caution, into the old dusty receiver. For a few seconds there was no response from the other end, and then I heard Harry's voice, although hardly heard would have been more accurate.

'I had lunch with your father—'

'Yes, I know. I saw you on to the bus, remember?'

'I'm afraid he poisoned me.'

I was speechless for a few seconds.

'He wouldn't poison you, Harry, only Russians and Italians poison people,' I said with some authority.

'Just a – a bad joke – to go with the bad mussel. I did as you said and followed him in whatever he ordered, so the wines matched even though I hate mussels. Got back just in time for Dermot to call the doctor. He had to give me an injection – the doctor, not Dermot – to stop me being sick.'

After which the phone went dead. My imagination became one of those flies you can never swat without falling out of the window.

After locking up all the security files, which took forever, I caught a taxi.

Harry was back in his half of the room, looking not so much pale as greenish-white, almost as if his complexion had taken on the colour of the sea to fit in with the mussels.

'I am so sorry, Lottie-bags, made a titty-poo of myself.' Harry smiled bravely. 'He was very nice, your father, and dropped me back here, which was when I started to be Uncle Dick.'

'I should have known he would choose mussels or oysters or something like that – oh, dear.'

I patted Harry's hand in a lame kind of way and continued to visit him for the next few days, at the end of which Harry was recovered, but Dermot certainly was not.

A few evenings later he beckoned me to go into the kitchen with him. He closed the door, which was unfortunate because he had just bought kippers and they were sitting on the grill pan waiting to be cooked, and I thought they were eyeing me, which was almost worse than the way Dermot was eyeing me. In fact, it seemed to me that the kippers were looking at me in a more kindly fashion. Actually, by the time Dermot had finished accusing me of ruining Harry's life, I almost envied the kippers their future in the grill pan.

'Since Harry fell ill he has changed beyond recognition. He is like that painter – Augustus John – after he knocked his head in the sea.'

I frowned. I had not noticed that Harry had changed that much. Very well he was a little paler, very well he was a little careful of himself, but when last seen he was out and about and finding himself some clean socks, which was huge for Harry.

'Do you know what he wants to do now?'

I shook my head.

'Get even better?' I ventured.

'No, no, this is nothing to do with his health, no. This is political. He wants to become a communist!'

I knew then why my heart had sunk when Harry had kept saying that my father was so kind. My father was brilliant with his agents. They all said, time and again, how kind he was – so if Harry had told Dermot that he wanted to become a communist, that must mean that Harry had agreed to work for my father undercover, like Melville and Hal. The first thing you had to do was to go about spouting Marx to all your friends – although Melville and Hal had not taken that line, on account of the kind of specialised work they did. Besides, no one would have believed them. They took the *Daily Telegraph* into rehearsal and voted Conservative so they could go on getting parts as officers and gentlemen in war films and plays.

'Oh, dear,' I said, averting my eyes from the kippers. 'Oh, dear, oh, dear, oh, dear. That is a change of character.'

'Exactly, just like that great painter Augustus John who went from being a nice shy boy to a raving sex maniac.'

'But a very talented one,' I said, because I always try to look on the bright side when I am around Dermot, for all sorts of reasons.

He shook out his copy of the *Manchester Guardian* at me. I knew what the shake meant. It meant that he might be left-wing himself but he drew the line at communism.

Happily, Dermot's attention had now switched to the poor kippers, so I was able to sidle out of the kitchen, close the door and bolt off to find Harry.

'Coffee?'

He nodded happily. Once we were in the noisy coffee bar we were able to talk frankly, which is not something I like doing. But I knew that if what Dermot had said was true, matters must now have become quite serious.

'So you are embracing communism.'

Harry nodded.

'It's all part of what you have to do if – you know – if you're working for you know what.'

'But your father is a member of the Sunningdale Golf Club; your mother is a pillar of the Church. What can possess you ever to think they will countenance your views?'

'Oh, they don't have to know, really they don't. Just enough to make them worried, but not too anxious, your father said. Enough to make them think that I am just going through a phase. For the moment I am only a volunteer at CPHQ. They're trying me out on little tasks.'

I knew that a great many agents, double or otherwise, had to convince their families that they were proper communists, but I supposed that in Harry's case my father was treading lightly to begin with, which was just as well since Harry was so good-natured it seemed to me that neither of his parents would believe him. They would probably think he was just having them on.

I went to work the next morning convinced that nothing would come of it, and nothing did seem to come of it until a few weeks later, weeks during which Harry did seem to change a bit although nothing outrageous – it was mostly a matter of costume. He started wearing collarless shirts and adopting a pair of what he imagined were Trotsky-style glasses, but which I thought made him look more Chekhov than communist.

As I say, other than that nothing much happened until one Saturday morning when I was going to take the Underground to meet Arabella for lunch, I passed a strange-looking figure standing outside the station. I did not do a double take – I did a triple take. The strange-looking figure was Harry and he was holding out copies of the *Daily Worker* to passers-by, most of whom happily ignored him.

'I'll take one,' I said, my eyes lowered.

'Thank you, miss.' Harry had assumed a Cockney accent that would have got him a part anywhere.

'Thank you, sir,' I said, taking my copy of the *Daily Worker* and attempting to be heavily sarcastic. Then I mouthed 'see you for coffee at six', which Harry ignored because someone had just kicked him on the shin and shouted 'bloody Russian' at him.

I had to leave him even though he was hopping about a bit clutching his ankle, or else his cover might have been blown.

I was pretty anxious about him, and when he turned up, very eventually, he was limping so badly my first thought was that he must be up for Richard III.

'Not funny, Lottie-bags, not funny at all. Really, the things people do to you if they think you're a communist.'

I sighed, but only inwardly.

'I suppose you know all about this undercover stuff, because of your father, ahem, ahem, ahem?' Harry asked.

'What I know could be fitted into an egg cup,' I said, with complete honesty. 'Actually I don't like all this undercover stuff – it makes me feel as if nothing is really true.'

Harry looked around to make sure there was no one too near us before pulling up his coat collar; presumably so no one could lip read what he had to say to me, although actually he shouldn't have bothered as our exchange was not all that interesting.

'What I have discovered is that communists are very, very boring,' he mouthed at me. 'They do not make jokes and, worst of all, don't laugh at anyone else's. Most of them have beards, which are hosts to goodness knows what, and they put cheap Biros behind their ears, and some of them don't even wash their shirts. I tell you, Communist Party HQ is what my father calls absolute hell.'

'Can't you give up all this now, before it's too late?'

'Not really.' Harry looked momentarily sad, but then he brightened. 'I have to do more to free our country from these people, Lottie, really I do, and besides your father has plans for me.'

Now my heart really did sink. I found myself praying: *O, dear Lord of all that is beautiful, keep Harry and plans away from each other.*

'What sort of plans?' I mouthed back at him.

'I don't know exactly. He wants me to meet him at Lord's Cricket Ground, carrying a copy of the *Daily Telegraph* and dressed in a suit.'

'But supposing you get a job?' I asked, speaking normally.

'That's all right,' Harry continued, still mouthing his words. 'If I get an acting job, fair enough, he says, but for the moment I must try harder selling the newspaper. I sold a couple today – one to your father, which was very good of him, I thought,' he added, brightly.

'Yes,' I agreed. 'Have you thought of changing your pitch?'

'No, apparently CPHQ are keen on me staying at the same old Ken High Street corner pitch, beside the chap pretending to be blind who is selling matches. He keeps lifting his shades to see how much he has snaffled.' Harry nodded. 'Yup. We've become quite friendly. I go and have tea with him at Lyons' Corner House and he tells me all about his life: how he had to take up begging on account of missing out on his army pension, his wife leaving him and so on. He's quite decorated, you know. You'd think he would be bitter, but he's not. He's as cheerful as you or I.'

I went back to Dingley Dell feeling thoughtful only to bump into Hal and Melville both hurrying back into the house carrying copies of the *Daily Worker*.

'Really, Lottie darling, the things I do for England,' Melville said, sighing.

'I shall read it cover to cover,' Hal boomed. 'I think of it as a political *Beano*. Apparently these asses really believe we are all equal. They wouldn't if they'd ever toured with Dougie Robinson.'

I went downstairs a few hours later to find Mrs Graham lighting the dining-room fire with several more copies of the wretched thing.

'Really can't see who would want to read such nonsense,' she murmured. 'Have to set fire to these before any visitors catch sight of them. Red rag to a bull it would be. Still,' she turned to look at the nicely laid table, 'we have Mr and Mrs Bernard Walters to dinner tonight, so that should brighten things up a bit.'

Bernard Walters was always in the newspapers; even I knew that he had the impresario's golden touch and a finger in every entertainment pie. I stopped halfway up the stairs on my way back to the drawing room, and then I went down again.

'I will be in for dinner tonight after all, Mrs G,' I told her.

'Very well. Put yourself where you want. Your mother being away, you can play hostess for her.'

I re-laid the table, carefully putting myself next to Mr Walters, and then I zipped upstairs to change.

In the drawing room I could hear animated voices, and Melville playing the piano, quietly, which my father liked him to do because he said it covered awkward moments, if there were any.

Mr and Mrs Walters were charming and evidently very rich in that unapologetic way that is so impressive to people like me. Their clothes, their wristwatches, jewellery and footwear, seemed to be staring out at the rest of us with pity. My father had several rich relations but they never looked like the Walters did. The relatives wore faded clothes, and very, very old jewellery, and their shoes and handbags all looked as if they should be in the Victoria and Albert Museum. The ladies often had monograms engraved on their handbag clasps, and the men's signet rings bore crests that were small and discreet; although their cigarette cases were gold, they were worn gold. So all in all, to me at least, the Walters were birds of paradise, a fresh breeze blowing in from the affluent West End where they had many shows running, shows that bankrolled their new venture into cinema.

I did not unveil my newly formed idea to Bernard Walters until halfway through dinner when everyone was very nicely thank you, because my father was always so generous with drinks that no one could stay completely sober for long – although tonight I had made a point of doing so. As it happened I had read Melville's latest film script, a Walters production, in case there was a part in it suitable for Harry – which at that moment there was not, but more of that anon.

'When are you due to start shooting the film Mr Walters?' I ventured, smiling with what I hoped was dedicated fascination at him.

'We start location shooting next week,' he said. 'Why, do you want a part?' he added, jokingly.

'No, very kind of you,' I said, sweetly, 'but I have no ambitions to be an actress.'

'What a relief for your father,' he said, laughing. I too laughed, although a trifle obediently.

'May I tell you a story?' I asked.

'By all means,' he said, but his eyes reflected the thought 'oh, dear'.

It didn't take long, as well it shouldn't since I had rehearsed and even timed it.

'My,' he said, after I had finished. 'That is such a good take on what we need in the script. We could start there.' He looked round the table. 'I can just see Melville particularly – and Hal, of course. Young lady, you have given me the start and the finish to my picture. A young officer dying in order to save them, and then for them to end up as they do ... brilliant!' he said, sighing happily. 'I love flashback. With flashback you know you can settle down, sit back, let the story unroll.'

After which I sat back and crossed my fingers.

Nothing untoward happened at Dingley Dell until a week or two later when I came back late from the coffee bar, but not just late, elated.

On what I suspected was my father's instigation, Harry had got a part in *Officers and Gentlemen*. Or, in his words, 'Went up for it, and only gone and got it, Lottie!'

'Apparently they've rewritten the script, and I have the featured part of a young officer, a big part, and what's more I die, Lottie-bags! Gus is over the moon. Doesn't understand how I got it, but apparently Bernard Walters asked for me, said he thought I had the right look – I am "touched with something tragic", he said. Anyway I have a big part, and I am going to have a hero's end.'

How changed the script now was, and how closely it resembled my suggestion to Bernard Walters, I did not appreciate until I walked into Dingley Dell's drawing room and found Melville playing the piano with Hal standing beside him, both of them looking dire.

'Something the matter?' I asked, nervously.

'Nothing that need trouble you, Lottie,' Hal boomed, while Melville played a very sad late-evening number.

'New pages for the film this morning. The script has been rewritten fore and aft. For the first five minutes Melville and I are unrecognisable – we are blind, practically limbless and selling matches door to door – crutches, the lot.'

'Well, that's quite good, isn't it?' I asked, tension going to my throat so much that I kept clearing it. 'I mean if you're in the start, and so on.'

'It means when the blasted flashback is over, young lady, no one will know who we are, don't you see? How will we register from the off in our bandages and dark-shaded glasses? We won't, is the answer, and registering at once is what we actors – we *stars* – are all about.'

I knew this was what Gus called 'a lot of actors' *abble dabble*'.

'Oh, I expect it will all turn out for the best. People will like discovering that it was really you, later on in the picture,' I said, carelessly.

Hal shook his head.

'That is such a civilian's remark.'

To be a 'civilian' in theatrical terms means you are tantamount to being a complete outsider. I felt duly put down, but not as much as I should because I was a tiny bit proud of my suggestion having been taken up by Bernard Walters.

Even so I climbed the stairs to bed feeling a bit dreadful. My take on the script, my idea for the start of the film that had been prompted by Harry's friend the match-seller, was to show the many dire results of the war, the gallant officers abandoned by the country they had served so bravely. The story had been planted in my head by what Harry had told me about his heroic old soldier friend now being forced to sell matches outside Ken High Tube Station.

But, of course, I could not leave it there. I had to find out whether my father had pulled a string or seven to get Harry seen for the part of the young officer.

'Not really,' he said, staring into the drinks cupboard, which was always his way when he was being modest and at the same time definitely not going to admit to anything. 'Although I did have a problem with Harry and the newspaper-selling. One of my people was selling matches at the next-door pitch, and he said Harry spent too much time talking to him and giving him tea at Lyons' Corner House, and CPHQ were moaning that sales were down – communists as you know are money mad. Still, all better now that Harry has a part. Get things going for him. Bernard Walters is a good chap.'

As soon as my father said someone was a 'good chap', I knew what it meant. It meant that Bernard Walters was one of his people. I made my father promise not to let Harry know anything about the dinner.

Further conversation revealed that the chap selling matches was invaluable to my father. The boxes often contained code numbers and messages, but handed only to the right people, of course – and now that the match-seller had become part of the inspiration for the start of a feature film, I felt quite proud.

Harry had the last word, finally. He was looking thoughtful the next time we met.

'I think the heroic look that impressed Bernard Walters, Lottie, was because of me being kicked outside Ken High Tube Station. I think that is how it came about.' He brightened. 'I don't have to be a communist anymore, your father says. Just report to him if I notice anything about someone, be a sort of part-time communist watchdog, on the lookout.'

'Sounds like a better thing,' I said, looking diplomatic, which was difficult for me. 'I don't suppose you'll miss it – selling the *Daily Worker*?'

'No, but I did one thing you'll like – to celebrate getting the part, I bought up the whole tray of matches from that nice chap. Want some? He tried to stop me but I insisted.'

'The whole tray?'

'Yes. Do take some, Lottie. I don't need matches, we don't have a fire at the flat.'

So that was why I staggered home with a load of matches, for who knew what was hidden in the boxes?

The following morning I presented them to my father, who sighed, and walked off to a waiting taxi with a string bag full of them.

Sometimes it seemed to me that running agents was a lot more complicated than people realised.

THE INSECURITY FILE

It was not often that I saw Arabella looking worried, particularly not when she knew she had a nice chunk of leave coming up and wouldn't have to sit opposite me for a few days.

'What's up, Miss Tankerton?'

'Tankerton is not my surname, Lottie.'

'It is today, Tankers. It is so much your surname that I have posted it on the Section Board under "Miss A. Tankerton, missing believed lost".'

'Not funny, Lottie.'

'No, I know, not funny, Arabella, just a way of getting your attention by annoying you.'

'I can't talk to you here.'

'You always talk to me here.'

'Not about this I don't.'

Again it was not often that Arabella abandoned her expression of yogi-like calm and turned her eyes towards the fire exit. The usual sphinx-like look was missing from her large brown orbs as I followed her out on to the fire escape under the pretext of having a cigarette. This was considered highly unorthodox in any other Section, but our bosses were delightfully indulgent on this issue on account of the fact that it kept everyone happy; even the ladies in files enjoyed the odd roll-up on a mild afternoon.

'Don't lean backwards, Lottie, you'll set off alarms in the whole building.'

I stepped forward and half-shut the security door to the hallway, leaving my foot propped up to keep it open.

I turned and looked longingly at the relevant switch. What a thing to be able to do – empty the whole building with one little touch. I imagined all the files being hurled into the filing cabinets, all the safes being quickly locked, but most of all the tight expressions of the MI5 officers and policemen as they imagined either the Russians pouring through the building, or a fire raging. It would certainly break up the rhythm of the day. I knew Commander Steerforth would quite enjoy it, on account of having been in the navy where those sorts of things always seemed to keep happening on account of the Admiralty being full of people who really had never ever been to sea. In fact, Commander Steerforth once told me, in strictest secrecy of course, that several highly decorated admirals could not even see an ocean wave without calling Hughie.

'It's happened, Lottie.'

'What's happened, Arabella?'

Something must have been terribly wrong because we were never this formal, repeating each other's names like people do when trying not to forget them, and Arabella looking positively wild-eyed.

'You know Section XXX? Above us?' She pointed upwards.

Of course I knew it. Section XXX were toffee-nosed, super-triple-vetted, and most of them highly seasoned, having spent large chunks of their lives in fascinating places looking for well-placed husbands. Or else – or so the rumour went – having raging affairs with persons in high places. The gossip alone gave them a kind of cachet among us lower orders – the combination of travel and rumoured love affairs meant they were properly sophisticated. Added to which, a little like East End criminals who wear lots of heavy gold rings to denote how many hits they have carried out, many of these ladies wore jewellery made of what Commander Steerforth called 'fool's gold'. I had never met any of them formally but I had often shared the lift with them, and was amazed by their aura of languid sophistication and constant references to what sounded like 'Singa-ore' or 'Ma-layah'. The half-swallowed words made abroad seem even further away.

So now I had clued into Section XXX it was time to listen to what was giving Arabella indigestion.

'The *thing* has been sent for by XXX.'

I could feel myself losing colour, truly I could. It was not possible, surely?

We had to refer to the wretched little account I had written about being in MI5 as 'the thing' because it was full of Top Secret material. Well, not really Top Secret, but what the authorities would consider Top Secret. And worse than that it was full of jokes, and we all knew how well jokes about MI5 would go down with MI5, especially if Special Branch heard them. I mean, talk about Arsenal versus Chelsea – that was Special Branch and MI5.

As for the likelihood of my jokes being appreciated at home, it would be more likely to find my father voting communist. The thought of him discovering what I had done made me want to sit down, but of course I couldn't because I was holding the fire exit open with my foot while pretending to smoke a cigarette at the same time.

'We've got to keep calm.'

This was getting worse and worse. Arabella never appealed for calm. She was calm itself in human form. She could have taught Gandhi calm.

'We have to keep calm and make a plan.'

I liked the bit about the plan so much I smoked my cigarette properly, and shortly after started to feel quite sick.

Arabella regarded me with something close to spite, as well she might. It was all my fault in the first place for writing the book-thing, and making jokes about the security service, and then putting it in a file that we both were quite sure at the time would go straight to Kew and never be found again until Kingdom Come when it might make people laugh.

'Of course, it was Rosalie's file, really,' Arabella suddenly said, frowning. 'So what if we sent for it ahead of XXX? I mean, I could tell her I sent in the wrong file accidentally and we need to re-do the thing – not your thing, the real thing, the file.'

She paused and stared at me, calm returning to her aura.

'Why did you write it up in the first place, Lottie, all the doings that went on here? I have temporarily forgotten.'

'I dunno,' I said, assuming a Just William voice, which I can do sometimes when in a quandary. 'I suppose I thought it would be fun for posterity to read.'

Arabella gave me another pitying look.

'Posterity won't be interested in MI5 and all our doings here. They will be too busy watching their laundry going round in their washing machines.'

'They might be,' I said, and stopped using my Just William voice because Arabella didn't find it funny. 'I mean sometimes people are interested in funny things.'

The look Arabella gave me was the one Mrs Brown might give William when his socks were covered in mud.

'Ah.'

Arabella stubbed out her cigarette very carefully on a penny, and we both thankfully stopped smoking, which we hated anyway and only did when we wanted a private talk on the fire escape.

'I know someone in XXX,' she said, suddenly. 'Zuzu Smith-Brown.'

'Is she a nice-ish sort of person?'

'Zuzu is like no one else you have ever met, she really is, but she might do.'

There wasn't enough time for me to be curious. We had to get to this Zuzu person in what Commander Steerforth called 'naval time'.

Arabella indicated that the best way to get her was by making an arrangement that would intrigue her. A hand-written invitation to an art exhibition was settled on.

It felt more than strange and even a little terrifying to be in the same position as, say, a double agent, and I know that even Arabella was feeling less than happy about what we were doing, but it had to be done this evening before the file could be brought back from Kew on the electric shuttle used by MI5 personnel and files – or they might just as well be returning from Never Never Land for all we knew; except in our case the file seemed to be coming back before you could say 'Tinkerbell' or that you believed in fairies.

So there we were, pretending to be smart in a well-known art gallery.

'Ah, there she is,' Arabella said in a low voice. Something I've noticed if paintings are frightful and not at all what people would ever stick on their own walls, they always talk in low voices. It is almost as if they feel by keeping their voices at church level they will be able to escape from them quicker.

Zuzu turned out to be so Section XXX that she was almost too good to be true. She was tall, tanned, blonde-streaked, with those long thin arms that are always lightly tanned so as to show off fine blonde hairs and slim gold wristwatches.

Arabella indicated the exit door as soon as was possible, but not before Zuzu said to the gallery owner, 'I'll be back – they are wonderful.' Which of course she didn't mean but he was obviously thrilled if only by her smile.

'Have you ever seen such a tatty talent?' she asked rather too loudly before we had quite got through the doors to the street outside. 'Come with me, I will drive you home.'

We followed her obediently to her car, which I walked past only to be caught by the arm and pulled back to it.

'Here we are, here's Rollo,' she said, laughing. 'Rollo, meet Arabella and Lottie.'

Rollo was an old Rolls-Royce. Arabella, who knew everything about cars, immediately lit up and murmured his details. She even knew the date he was manufactured. There was just time enough for me to be impressed before

I climbed in and sat back, lost in admiration for the old motor's gorgeous interior. Just like Arabella, Zuzu already seemed to me the sort of girl who was everything I could never be.

And now she turned out to be even more so as she drove the old Rolls through traffic lights, shouting to us: 'I'm colour blind! Tell me, is that green?'

She seemed too good to be true. From that moment on I felt that somehow or other she would be a great ally and that the dreaded file would be found and my stupid little account of life at MI5 with it, and everything would turn out better than expected.

At the coffee bar we made a plan. Zuzu would look out for the file. The moment it came into her Section she would pounce on it and sweep it off to a safe place where no one would find it.

'Not the lift shaft again?' Arabella moaned, referring to an incident in our Section when a previous incumbent – Laetitia – who before leaving England, and just as well, dropped a number of files down the lift shaft on the sound reasoning that no one in MI5 would ever look there.

'Oh, I think so, don't you?' Zuzu said, stoutly. 'After all, it works, and as we all know, if something works you do it. It is the first rule of the military, isn't it? That's why they have all those code words, so they act but don't think. Thinking is not something the military are allowed to do.'

Arabella was starting to look bored, so I quickly suggested a plan for signalling the arrival of the dreaded 'thing'. Arabella, as I remembered, had secured it into the back of a particularly thick file.

'Why didn't you burn it?' Zuzu wanted to know.

'Posterity,' Arabella said, briefly, before ordering another coffee. 'We thought it would be funny to have it found in fifty years' time so that everyone would know what it was really like to be in MI5 in our here and now.'

'Oh, I know, like those tins and bottles people bury under buildings and trees.'

Zuzu lit a cigarette.

'We just don't understand the sudden need for the file,' Arabella mused. 'It's not your Section staff.'

'I know.' Zuzu nodded and blew a superb cigarette ring before continuing. 'It's probably Major Jones-Littleton. He will ask for things from Kew, or Scotland, or heaven only knows where. I wouldn't be surprised if he asked for the Crown Jewels to be sent from the Tower. If he thinks he is on the trail of something, he is a nightmare. I could never even mention the lift shaft to him; he would have the bottom of it swept in no time at all.'

It was then that I thought I saw a look come into Arabella's eyes, a look that I did not like to see. It was the look of a person who has had a great thought. Myself, I am all for avoiding great thoughts; if you look at the history of the world people having great thoughts always seems to lead to trouble. I mean think about it. A glass of wine and thou beside me in the wilderness – that is a nice small thought, but make it bigger and it becomes – yes, but what *kind* of wine? And whose wilderness *is* it? And do the Council know you have planted that tree?

However, Arabella's big thought did not come to fruition until later. And it seemed that it was Zuzu's cigarette that had prompted it.

We were on the fire escape again, pretending to have a gasp of nicotine, when Arabella eyed me with intent, never an easy moment. Have you ever imagined Gandhi eyeing you? Well, no, of course not, and I will say it might have been a bit different and all, but even so that kind of eyeing of you can make you feel strangely unable to think about anything except what the person in possession of those eyes wants of you.

'I have worked out a plan,' Arabella began. 'It is actually quite simple.'

Here again, like great thoughts, I have a fear of simple plans, because if you think about it, no plan is ever really simple. It just appears so to the person possessed of the great thought.

'We haven't had a fire drill since you came to the Section, have we?'

I had to agree we had not.

'And you know how Commander Steerforth loves a bit of excitement and doesn't really get much? So why don't you suggest to him that he sends a memo to Head of All Sections to suggest a fire drill? That way we can get Zuzu to hand us the file, we can chuck the 'thing' down the lift shaft, and hand back the file when she returns. All tickety-boo.'

I must admit, I was lost in admiration. So much so that I was sorely tempted to lean back and set off the fire alarm straight away. However, we had to get Zuzu to agree first, which of course she readily did.

'Superb, Arabella, just give the word.'

Commander Steerforth was as thrilled with the idea of a fire drill as we had hoped. He took over the whole proceedings with élan, charm, and the kind of enthusiasm that could have had the whole world dancing the Sailors' Hornpipe.

As soon as possible all Sections were informed. We were put on alert, and everyone became really rather excited because no one had caught any spies lately and everyone was privately wondering whether we ever would again. A general alarm should ginger things up a bit.

Zuzu as expected came to the fore. She was ready with the dratted file, and Major Jones-Littleton so busy seeing to his security arrangements that she later said she could have walked out of the building with a whole set of security keys, let alone the file.

It was thrilling to see everyone rushing about doing what they had to do, and all the ladies in files saying it was so exciting and reminded them of the Blitz, and everyone pulling together. Zuzu zipped up and down the stairs and the wretched 'thing' joined the other causes of embarrassment that had been thrown down the lift shaft by Laetitia. So it had all worked to Arabella's plan ... except that when Zuzu zipped back upstairs again, sliding the file out of sight on top of a cabinet, Major Jones-Littleton was waiting for her at her desk. It seemed that on doing a spot check to see that everything tallied with what had been there before the fire drill began, he had noticed the file missing from her tray.

At that moment in time I would have joined the other files in the damp darkness below the lift, but not Zuzu. She squared up to the Major, or so at least we gathered later.

'What did you say?'

Zuzu smiled as she recounted this and lit a cigarette, which she enjoyed for a couple of puffs before taking up the story again.

'I told him that he was on the wrong track. That the file he had been on about getting out of Kew was a total waste of time, and I knew this because my uncle was a general who had been on that particular trail and it had ended in a no-go area, which not even our dear Prime Minister would breach ... and we all know what a success he has been, don't we? So I told him I had hurried the embarrassing thing straight back to Kew before someone realised he had hooked it out.'

'Did he buy that?'

'Of course. Majors have a fear of generals that never leaves them.'

'Who is your uncle, this famous general?' Arabella asked, because I was half-frozen with admiration and could find no words.

'I have no idea, darling, none at all,' Zuzu said, smiling. 'But I expect I will find one soon.'

Arabella's eyes assumed their normal sphinx-like state. Seeing this, I knew we were home and dry. As long as Arabella had that look I felt our little world was safe, and so it seemed it was, until Zuzu added one more thing, that extra bon mot I did not want to hear.

'By the way, I thought it such a shame to throw away your account of life in MI5, never mind the file.'

'It's been nothing but a pain.' I shuddered.

'Now come on, I want to buy us all a glass of champagne at my club and then off we will go to dinner. I know a little place in Kew. Rollo can take us, and we can all drink to state secrets and enjoy ourselves. Joy and life and laughter... that is what it is all about.'

So that is what we did. We drank to fire drills and fictitious generals, then Arabella, possibly exhausted from all the excitement, decided to take some leave and go to Paris for no better reason than to see if it was still there. I knew what she meant. Places can be like a tracing of a drawing. As long as it is still on the tracing paper, it is fine, but when you try to put it back down again over the original, it never quite fits. But at any rate she was taking her mother, and they were going to see an elderly aunt who lived in splendid bohemian isolation near the Sacré Coeur, from whence she had never been known to descend on account of all the steps.

'You and Zuzu can stay at the flat while we're gone,' Arabella offered. 'Nearer to Harrods for Zuzu.'

'She really prefers Fortnum and Mason.'

'Well, tough, then.'

As soon as Monty – permanent person-of-all-work at the Knightsbridge flat – met Zuzu he fell in love. She was just his sort of person. He called her Mademoiselle, and of course Zuzu loved him, especially the wig that he was in the habit of raising when he was thinking.

'Oh, Monty, your tiny, tiny drop scones would send most people to paradise.'

'Mademoiselle is too kind.'

Everything about Zuzu had Monty entranced. Her habit of leaving Rollo without petrol, with a notice on the windscreen saying 'Gone out'. Her love of flowers, which extended to filling the whole flat with blossoms costing an unearthly amount. Her insistence on taking me nightly to shows, even ones she knew were dreadful, teaching me how to go to the gallery, watch for an empty seat in the stalls and then, as the lights were lowered, dash down and sit in it.

'So much nicer for the actors to see the front rows filled, don't you think?'

But all the time, both Monty and I knew that Zuzu's days with us were numbered, for she was once more off to foreign parts, on behalf of the War Office.

'If you see a war has broken out, you will know it's me,' she told us as she kissed us goodbye at London Airport.

Monty and I watched her plane mounting into the skies and Monty raised his wig in au revoir to his dear, glamorous Mademoiselle.

'If only there were more people like Mademoiselle in the world,' he said sadly as he drove the Rolls back to Knightsbridge. 'I shall look after Rollo for her as if he was my own,' he added. 'Not a day will go by when I don't polish him.'

Later on, I met Harry at our usual coffee bar.

'So Zuzu's gone?' he said, trying not to look relieved.

'Yes,' I said, not able to keep the sadness out of my voice. I sighed.

'And nothing nice is ever going to happen to you again?'

'Oh, of course it will, but let's face it, some people do colour the room they are standing in with rather a special aura, don't they?'

It was Harry's turn to look sad. 'I wish I did.'

'You do,' I said, but at the same time I couldn't help thinking that neither of us did.

*

Happily Arabella came back from Paris able to report it was still there, and was fascinated by everything new I had to tell her about Zuzu. There was so much, and I thought I did rather well, but Arabella had that extra perception some sphinx-like people did.

'You're missing her and all the excitement,' she said.

I nodded. It was true.

'How did you know?'

'You should see Monty,' she said, shortly. 'Talk about depressed. He spends all his spare time polishing that old jalopy of hers and mopping his eyes with a duster.'

I knew how Monty felt. Zuzu was a comet, and now all we could see was the white trail across our lives where she had been.

'You know what,' Arabella stated, a few days later, 'you and Harry should get together.'

'We are together,' I said, and it was my turn to be short.

'No, I mean, you should write together. After all, he is always trying to write things and you are always trying to write things. You should be like those Hollywood couples in the thirties – the Hacketts and all the others. Start scribbling together.'

The clouds seemed to lift for me at this suggestion, but when I passed it on to Harry he looked less than enthused.

'We don't write at all the same way. We would be like Thing and Yang.'

'Exactly,' I said, happily. 'That is why it will work. Come on, sit down opposite me.'

'Please, Lottie, it's a bit early for that.'

I had bought some Woolworth jumbo pads and some Biros. Harry regarded these with extra suspicion.

'What shall we write about?'

I looked at him.

'What everyone our age writes about, Harry – ourselves or else about something that has happened to us – you know. Like when you had to sell the *Daily Worker* outside Ken High Underground to help my father out – that kind of thing.'

It seemed to make him happy, and that certainly made me happy, and some weeks into our new situation it seemed Arabella noticed how light my step was, and how much more often I smiled and laughed.

'So it's going all right – you and Harry?'

I nodded.

'Good.' She put down the book she was reading. 'Do you know, there's a chapter for every stage of your life in this,' she said, with some satisfaction.

I glanced down at the book. She was re-reading *The Wind in the Willows,* which she did every few months. It was her Bible.

I saw her smiling with some complacency as she closed it. 'Zuzu is very like the wayfarer rat, isn't she?'

I nodded again. The wayfarer rat, as we both knew, had made Ratty restless for his friend's life of adventure with his talk of faraway lands and strange peoples, for the sights and sounds of a different world. Zuzu had made Monty and me restless. Mole's solution for Ratty had been to get him writing.

'All better now then,' Arabella stated, and as I hurried off to catch the number nine bus and start work that evening with Harry, I could not but agree.

SUNDAY LUNCH

I had just taken a chunk of leave from the War Office to allow Harry and me to spend more time on our mutual writing career. This meant we were working day and night together, and getting to know each other better too.

There is nothing like staring across a small table at someone else who is stuck to realise what intimacy truly is. When stuck we also went for long walks – to get air into our brains, we said.

We were coming back from just such a walk in the Park before going on to Dingley Dell for lunch when Harry had a thought.

'If I was an alien sitting on my planet looking at this planet we inhabit, I think I know just when I would invade.'

I glanced at Harry. He was wearing his Sketchley's suit and a tie and shirt that looked newly pressed, but I knew from my father's point of view Harry might as well be from another planet on account of the length of his hair. Harry had short hair, but he did not have my father's generation's idea of short hair, which was short back and sides, primed and ready to join the services – although not the RAF.

My father and I had talked about this.

'He's a nice enough young man, Lottie. Just wish he would get his hair cut. I mean any minute now it could touch his collar.'

'That is short for nowadays, how he has it.'

'Never let him into the Regimental Mess.'

'He can't go around looking like you,' I said with sudden asperity. 'If he did no one would let him into rehearsal.'

My father looked at me in astonishment. I did not always sound so short, but I certainly felt short at that moment, and obviously sounded it.

'I see what you mean,' he said, eventually. 'You mean horses for courses?'

'Exactly,' I said, trying not to imagine Harry turning up at rehearsals looking like my father. Everyone would think he had climbed into costume too early. 'As it is,' I continued, still feeling short on this issue, 'having his hair cut for that film he did with Melville and Hal has put him out of the running for a whole range of other parts. He has to let it grow again.'

'Not too long, I hope,' my father murmured, heading off for the garden, but before he did he turned back to me. 'I've learned something today,' he murmured, before he lit a pipe and started to stare at his favourite shrub, which judging from his expression also needed a haircut.

Back to Harry, still musing about planets and aliens, neither of which, I am afraid, held the slightest interest for me because I found catching a bus, or trying to understand how the telephone worked quite enough.

'The time to invade ...' he said, eyes dreamy with inspiration. 'The perfect time to invade is when they are eating their Sunday lunch. Think about it, Lottie. At some time or another, people are sitting down to Sunday lunch. The Italians preparing their ragùs, the French their casseroles, the British their roasts – all these people with their thoughts fixed on nothing but food, so that is the time to invade a country – when they're enjoying Sunday lunch!'

I might have been lost in admiration but after a long walk and talking playwriting in the Park, all I could think of was Mrs Graham at Dingley Dell busy cooking roast beef and Yorkshire pudding, and her special roast potatoes done till crispy with lashings of dripping.

'Come on, Shakespeare, time to face others of your profession.'

Sunday lunch at Dingley Dell might well be a prime target for invading aliens, but for me it was just as life should be, what with the cooking smells drifting up, and

Melville playing the old songs my father so liked, and my mother engaged in a heated defence of the proscenium arch in theatre and Hal booming on about the glories of the apron stage.

For some reason Hal's booms always started with 'my dear lady', which my mother had complained to him made her feel as if she were wearing a crinoline. But her pleading always fell on deaf ears, so perhaps that was how Hal thought of her.

As Harry and I went into the drawing room there was the sound of a definite boom coming from Hal and as usual it was about the theatre, with my mother complaining that there was nothing on in the West End to tempt people like her to buy a seat in the stalls.

'Well now, there is a solution – get more people like you to write suitable plays, my dear lady.'

Hal's expression was one of settled contentment, what with the music and the smell of the beef cooking, until he saw Harry, and then his face fell. Well, I say 'fell', to explain how his expression changed to something very close, I imagine, to the expression of someone who had just been told he had lost all his money in a Stock Exchange crash.

'Enter the Fallen Hero,' Hal boomed at Harry.

Fallen Hero was a reference to Harry's part in the film they had all just been shooting, a small but showy role that might have been a great opportunity for him, and indeed for Hal and Melville had the film not run into post-production difficulties, which meant none of them could benefit from it until it was shown.

'Hallo, Hal,' Harry muttered, and I could see that he was making a terribly big effort not to scowl, because, as I remembered yet again, he knew Hal and Melville resented his being cast in the picture mainly because Harry died a glorious death in it and they didn't. Also he was seen at the front of the film in a dream sequence which meant that he could rush about without bandages, which was great for Harry, at any rate we thought so. Even though the film had not yet been shown we had great hopes for it, and Harry's part in it. However just at that moment both Hal and Melville turned and frowned at Harry, making it quite plain that they hoped he would get through Sunday lunch with my father and mother without opening his mouth except to post roast beef in it.

Now if there was one thing Harry found difficult it was obfuscating. He had always felt it his public duty to make a case for something – well, anything really. I had warned him not to make any of his statements at lunch, it was just not done at Dingley Dell, and I have to say for Harry that from the moment we sat down to lunch, his behaviour was beyond reproach. He smiled and passed things, and nodded, and was altogether angelic until my father turned to ask him what he was working on.

Harry looked vague, which was the right tactic, but then he looked trapped in the headlights of my father's penetrating 'you had better tell me the truth, young man' gaze.

'How do you mean, sir? I have no acting work at the moment, not until the film comes out.'

Harry had paled a little round the edges, though until that moment he had been flushed from the impact of a pre-lunch sherry.

'Yes, everyone's in the same boat, I gather.' My father's penetrating gaze momentarily embraced the other two actors at the table. 'I was interested in what you and Lottie might be writing about? The subject of all the feverish meetings at your Earls Court flat.'

Oh, dear, I always hated my father being interested in anything to do with me; it made my toes scrunch because he could never avoid that slight tone of menace. It seemed if you used menace and implied threat in your day-to-day work, some of it still lingered, even over Sunday lunch.

'Well, sir, Lottie and myself – you know Lottie, don't you, sir?'

'We have met – from time to time.'

For some reason at that moment everyone else stopped talking. There was a ripple of laughter at my father's little joke.

'Lottie and I are working on a comedy together.'

'A comedy forsooth?' boomed Hal. 'You are brave souls indeed.'

'Yes,' Harry agreed, nodding.

My toes quickly undoubled as I attempted to kick Harry under the table. I realised too late that I had missed Melville saying 'ow' very loudly, at the same time as Harry had announced the title of our comedy – *The Happy Communist*.

'*The Happy Communist*, you say?' My father lingered over the words as if it was a secret message sent during the war to SOE. He then repeated the title several times, looking from me to Harry and back again as if he had just discovered we were double agents.

'Now there's a notion,' boomed Hal, laughing. 'So you're busy writing fantasy fiction, eh?'

My mother stared across the table at me, and I could see her thinking that she was right: it was high time I stopped going out with this unsuitable person called Harry.

'And this is a comedy, you say?'

Harry nodded miserably. He could do miserable nods better than most. 'Yes, sir. You see, Lottie and I ... that is, Lottie and myself ... we thought it would be fun to show that you could be a communist and have a sense of humour too.'

'It's a satire actually,' I said, quickly.

'Satire closes Satire-days,' Hal and Melville chortled together.

'The English never understand satire anyway,' my mother said, weighing in. 'They like their comedy broad.'

'We haven't got very far,' Harry said. 'Just early days, making our way. Probably won't finish it.'

'Probably just as well, probably time for the script to hit the wastepaper basket,' my father said shortly. 'Communism is not a funny subject.'

Lunch continued but everyone knew that a clanger had been dropped. Afterwards Harry and I walked round to his flat in silence.

'You might have said something else. You might have lied,' I said, at last.

'Oh, yes, so what could I have said?'

'You could have said *The Happy Commander*, or *The Happy Commodore*, or *The Happy* – well, anything.'

'I could,' Harry conceded, 'but I didn't.' He stared ahead miserably as we walked. 'I ruined lunch, didn't I?'

'No, of course not,' I told him. 'It gave them all something to talk about.'

'Your father didn't look at me after that. You can't blame him; he thinks we're making fun of his work – that at least was evident.'

'We're not, we're just writing about when you worked for him and all that – using your experiences selling the *Daily Worker*. I think we should go on with it, I do really.'

Harry took his front door key out of his pocket.

'I don't think we can. I mean, did you see your father's face? He didn't shake my hand when we left, just walked off into the garden.'

'Oh, he gets like that about communism, but he soon gets over it once he sees greenfly on his roses or a slug on his hostas. Besides, if we sell the script, he might be pleased. He might like it. He might enjoy us satirising communists, laughing at them because they're such a bunch of humourless Stalinist toadies.'

'And he might not, and we might both end up somewhere we might not want to end up – on an exchange visit to Siberia.'

The trouble was we had very few other ideas at that time. After casting around for somewhere to start, *The Happy Communist* had seemed like a gift, because we were writing about what had actually happened to Harry, and writing from experience is always the best course.

At my insistence we continued with *The Happy Communist*, and what is more we finished it and showed it to Harry's agent, Gus, who showed it to his partner who handled scripts, and when I say handled, he really did handle them – after Dewi had read them, or rather mauled them, they looked as if they had been rescued from a litter bin.

'It reeks,' Dewi announced, happily.

'That's only because you keep smoking over it,' Harry protested.

'No, dear boy, it reeks of talent.' He beamed at us across the table in the restaurant he'd invited us to. 'Dewi can sell this anywhere. I can. I haven't been so excited since I read – anything.'

'Or maybe something?'

'Quite right, since I last read something. With this in my hand I can walk in anywhere and have them reverberating with excitement.'

'I think we should get you a clean copy, without cigarette marks,' I ventured. 'If you are serious.'

'I have never been so serious since I first became an agent and there was a script waiting for me from Trevor Duncan. I was hardly out of my demob suit and there was the first Duncan on my desk ... and look what happened to him.'

'What did happen to him, this Trevor Duncan person?' I asked on the way home on the number nine bus.

'He went on to write all those films,' Harry said, at his most vague. 'That series, you know, about a window cleaner. *Up the Ladder*, *Down the Ladder*, *Crazy Ladder* – you know, all those.'

'They're not what we would want to do.'

'No, but they sold, and that is what we have to do. We have to sell this, Lottie.'

When Harry and I reached the flat Dermot was waiting for us on the other side of the front door, and his expression was less than welcoming. I saw at once that he had a copy of *The Happy Communist* in his hand. He smote it, there was no other word for it. He struck his hand across its rather impoverished exterior – no shiny cover, no special gold printing – and frowned at Harry.

'What are you doing with your life?'

Harry looked daunted, which was only understandable. 'How do you mean, Dermot?'

'What do you think I mean, Harry?'

This was a heavyweight advancing on a bantam. Not that Harry was especially small or anything, I should add quickly, but Dermot was in full fisticuffs mode. I thought I ought to say something before things went from beastly to quite ugly.

'Hmph,' I said, hoping this would calm things a bit. It didn't; in fact, it had the opposite effect.

'You have betrayed every Socialist principle that we have ever talked about in this script,' Dermot said, breathing hard.

I frowned. Last time there was a political dust up, Dermot, flat mate extraordinary, had found copies of *The Daily Worker* and accused Harry of being a lackey of the Communist Party. So what was he thinking?

'It's a comedy,' I said, stoutly. Actually I don't know quite how stoutly I said it, but I do know that the mention of our script being a comedy further inflamed Dermot. Even his nostrils flared.

'That,' he said coldly, and his voice was very cold, 'makes it much, much worse. In fact, that is what makes it a betrayal of all your values. Bernard Shaw would be ashamed of you.'

He emphasised 'your' in such a way that it was immediately plain to me that he knew I had none.

'Iz oo cross wiv us, Dermot?'

Harry was trying to lighten the atmosphere by doing his baby voice, which he only ever did when things were getting tough. Seeing that not even that was having an effect, he changed tack.

'Don't worry, Dermot, we won't sell it.'

'I'm sure we won't,' I added, at my creepiest.

But we did. Neither of us could believe it; we sold it to a film company whose offices were in Soho.

'They want to meet you. They love it,' Dewi shouted at us, stubbing out his thirtieth cigarette of the day. 'Off you go.'

Harry had an aversion to ladies with large chests so I had to cover his eyes as we passed the windows of Soho nightclubs until we reached the office of Chancy Pictures.

As we climbed the rickety staircase to their less than salubrious premises, I could not help wondering what my father would say, or even Harry's father – a long-time member of the Sunningdale Golf Club – and that was before we went in and sat down on the kind of chairs that my mother would put a hankie on before doing the same.

'I have to say, this is a great script,' Mr Chance told us, as he flicked a fly off his teacup. 'Dewi told me it was great, and it is great.'

I tried not to look at Harry. What was it with this first script we had written together that inflamed and enthused everyone so much? It was thrilling, but only for a second.

'Now to improve it …' Mr Chance continued.

'How do you mean?' Harry asked.

'Cup of tea?'

'We've just had one, thank you, Mr Chance,' Harry said, and pushed his chair back a little from the desk, as if the tea might be catching.

'It has so much in it that is good, but it needs more … more danger, more sex!'

Harry frowned. As the oldest person in our partner-ship he took it upon himself to speak up for our work.

'This is a satire, Mr Chance, and as such sex, as such, does not really pertain.'

'It should. We should have pertaining sex in it, and it will help the – yes, the satire. Make it much funnier. For instance, if he's selling the *Daily Worker* and a tart comes up to him and takes him off to her boudoir, she could be converted to communism by reading the newspaper. She could become convinced.'

Harry frowned. I could see him trying not to see that Mr Chance was not the right producer for *The Happy Communist*.

'You see, the flaw in this script is that the young man is not happy. We have to follow the title,' Mr Chance went on inexorably. '*The Happy Communist* means he should be happy, so that will mean we can have any amount of encounters of a sexual nature, finishing up with him becoming even happier, see?'

Harry could see he would not be right for Chancy Pictures. Even I could see that. He stood up and waved at Mr Chance from our side of the desk. I knew he was waving because he was worried about the teacup and the fly, and feeling a bit daisy about shaking Mr Chance's hand. Harry was a bit delicate like that. It was something we shared. We had both spent some time practising going in and out of public places using only our elbows on the door handles.

Back at the flat Dermot was drinking black tea from a mug left over from his time in the army. We both knew he was waiting for us to come through the door brimming with good news, which would be bad news for him. I looked at Harry. Harry looked at Dermot.

'Forgive me for saying this but there's something on your head.'

Dermot, resident hypochondriac at the flat, jumped to his feet and rushed over to the mirror.

'What? What is it? What do you mean?' He ran his hands through his hair.

Harry sighed.

'Well, if you can't see the two horns that have popped up on top of your head, Dermot baby, you need spectacles.'

Dermot did not find that funny. He snatched up his mug and retired to their room.

'I hope you haven't hurt his feelings,' I said as the door appeared to close behind him.

'Dermot doesn't have any feelings,' Harry said, with some relish.

'Yes, I do.' Dermot shouted back from their room.

'Dermot has big ears,' Harry went on smoothly. 'As well as horns that come out of his head and a long serpent's tail.'

'I am praying for you, Harry, and praying hard. I am praying that you are forced to sign a contract with the Shakespeare Memorial Theatre and spend a year wearing a toga and working for Wooden Top.'

'Needs must when the devil drives, Dermot old thing.'

The following day we went back to see Dewi to explain why we could not sell *The Happy Communist* to Mr Chance.

Dewi was difficult to see, not because he had a queue outside his office, but because he was hidden behind clouds of stronger-smelling smoke.

'I've taken my wife's advice and given up cigarettes,' he called happily from the other side of the
smog. 'She's right, cigarettes are bad for you. They lack
class. This is class.' He waved his cigar at us. 'Charlie
Chance just called and said you weren't happy with
the idea of adding sex to your film. You need sex,
Harry – you need sex, especially in a picture with the
word "happy" in it. Who can be happy in this world
without sex?'

'It's not that kind of property, Dewi.'

I stared in some admiration at Harry. He had never
used that word before about *The Happy Communist*.
'Property' gave it stature. I immediately grew a few
inches taller at the idea that I was co-writer not of a
film – but a property.

'Harry dear, a film does not become a property until
it is in the can, cast and filmed.'

'That always helps, of course.'

'And sex is always a requirement.'

'Unless they're aliens from outer space.'

I don't know why I said that, it must have been because
of Harry's fantasy about aliens landing all over the world
during Sunday lunch.

Both Harry and Dewi stared at me.

'Lottie dear, even aliens have sex,' Dewi said gently. 'I
think you'll find. They have to procreate.'

I shook my head, firmly.

'Recent research has proved that in the atmosphere where aliens live, they reproduce in a different way. It's like some fireflies have both male and female bits. It's the opposite on Mars where they don't have any bits at all. They do it by banging their heads together, apparently.'

'Why would they do that?' Dewi demanded, his expression serious, his tone indignant.

'To make more aliens,' Harry told him, his own expression equally serious.

'But not during Sunday lunch,' I offered.

'Well, fair enough, no one has sex during Sunday lunch,' Dewi conceded.

'So – do you want us to include aliens in *The Happy Communist*, to add that kind of sex?'

'It's not my Biro that's signing, Harry, not my Biro.'

'Well, we could try it, and see if it does the trick.'

Dewi smiled widely.

'My dears, I love triers. I will ring Charlie Chance, not mention aliens, just say that you're willing to try and insert sex and be back to him as soon as he can say Wardour Street.'

We left Dewi and went to a chemist where we bought some cheap scent and sprayed ourselves to get rid of the smell of cigars before staggering back to the flat, because walking does a great deal for shock.

'I don't know why you suggested aliens,' Harry kept saying.

'You brought aliens up, before Sunday lunch, remember?'

'Yes, but not to put into *The Happy Communist*.'

'It is quite clear that Mr Chance will not be interested unless we add some sex—'

Harry stopped striding up and down the sitting room and stared at me. 'Are you telling me that you will do anything for a sale?'

'Yup.'

'Even to the extent of adding aliens?'

'Yes.'

'Why?'

'Because once we have sold one property, we will go on to sell others. Look at any successful writer's career. You have to sell, you have to make money, and then gradually you're allowed to write what you want.'

'No wonder Dermot thinks you have contaminated me.'

'Now listen, Harry, love you as I do—'

He stared at me.

'As a writer and an actor,' I continued, carefully. 'I know we have to get on with this, we must just do it.'

'But how?'

'Easy,' I said firmly, determined on busking it. 'The happy communist is taken over by aliens when he is selling the *Daily Worker* on the Underground. They abduct him and his newspapers to Mars where they read them and, realising the error of their Martian capitalist ways, become communists themselves, while our hero returns to earth where he sets about teaching everyone at Communist Party Headquarters alien sex, i.e. banging their heads together. This dislodges all their brainwashing and the Communists end up laughing and making jokes.'

I had to admit that to me what I had just said sounded like the sort of film – sorry, property – Mr Chance would like. To my surprise, Harry actually quite liked it too.

So we set about it, but not without difficulty. Despite the fantasy about aliens having landed us in this situation in the first place, Harry found the script very hard going. He ate biscuits when things were difficult at work. We were on our ninth packet of Funky Dunkies by the time the young communists at CPHQ had started having sex by banging their heads and thereby dislodging their brainwashing – in the film, that is.

'I've had enough,' Harry announced when we'd finished, which was stating the obvious but it had been hard work. 'Now I to play golf with my father, you to the War Office and the dear Commander.'

'How's the scribbling going?' Arabella asked with an uninterested expression on her face as she wound what looked like a telephone book of A4 paper into her Underwood.

'So-so,' I said, before answering the telephone on my desk. I had thought it would be Commander Steerforth for me, but it was Dewi, obviously ringing me because Harry was golfing.

'My dear – good news. Charlie Chance has his Biro out. He wants the aliens *and* the communists. We have a sale, a contract! Now all we need are the stars.'

Harry and I met in the coffee bar to celebrate with spaghetti and a glass of wine.

'You were right, Lottie, better a sale than no sale. Now we have a film credit, we will be on our way.'

Mr Chance did indeed get his Biro out as Dewi had predicted, but the contract was so long and in such small print that Dewi must have skipped the boring bits because not much time had passed before he telephoned Harry to break the news, and what news it was.

'It's a big compliment in a way,' Harry tried to tell me.

'In what way?' I asked, coldly.

'In the way of, they are getting someone more famous than us – at the moment – to breathe on it.'

I stared at him.

'Who, Harry, who? Noël Coward?'

He cleared his throat. 'Not exactly, no. Trevor Duncan. He's had a string of hits – *Up the Ladder, Down the Ladder* – not our cup of tea, but they were very successful, Lottie.'

'I need to sit down,' I said.

'You are sitting down——'

'Are you telling me that Trevor Duncan is going to have top credit over us?'

'Oh, we'll still be there, on the credits, but he will have first credit. That's what they do in movies. They get scribblers like us to build the house, and then they get a more famous name in and he replaces the doorknocker and changes a light bulb and takes all the credit. That's the system.'

I stared right past Harry, which he never liked.

'Our first comedy credit has now gone to someone else,' I said, in a flat voice.

'It's still a credit,' Harry insisted.

'It won't be recognisable if that man gets his mitts on it,' I moaned.

'Look at it this way – at least your father won't get upset. Trevor Duncan told Dewi he's taking all the communism out of it, keeping the sex, and just having aliens.'

*

When I told Arabella she assumed her sphinx-like expression.

'Just as well you've kept your job here,' she stated, not feeling sorry for me at all.

'Anyway we've started on something else. Another comedy, no aliens, no communists – just two people who fall in love and start to write together.'

'Not terribly fictional then?'

'No, not at all. Just a goodly tale of life behind the typewriter.'

The following Sunday we did not go to Dingley Dell for lunch. We said nothing to each other, but we both knew that we would rather duck it, just in case my father had remembered why he was upset with us. Instead we cooked a roast lunch at the flat. I found it a long laborious business compared to lunch at Dingley Dell, what with peeling potatoes, and basting the meat, and while we made a pact to avoid making Yorkshire pudding, Harry made splendid gravy out of a packet of Bisto. There was so much on the table that I almost felt guilty there were only the two of us to eat it.

'Do you think we should ask Dermot in?'

'He is in, Lottie.'

'Well, do you think we should ask him into the kitchen to eat with us?'

'I wouldn't go near Dermot at the moment, Lottie-bags – he's got a terrible headache, he's living on Aspirin.'

'Oh, poor Dermot, why so?'

'I saved this up to tell you.' Harry paused in slicing the beef. 'I gave him the rewrite of The Happy Communist, and he's been rehearsing Martian sex ever since, in case he goes up for it. You should hear the head-banging. He's very method like that.'

Harry smiled contentedly as I only just avoided doing the elephant trick with my wine.

'What about Dermot's principles?'

'He said it was different now there are no communists in the script. Oh, and they've changed the title – it is now called *Sexy Aliens*.'

'*Sexy Aliens*? So still a satire then?'

'At least we have a cheque with Biro marks on it.'

'We do, and it hasn't bounced, so let's drink to sexy aliens.'

So we did, and then Harry had some more gravy – well, we both did – it was that good.

THE SHALLOW END

My mother was looking worried. 'Your father is looking worried.' Just for a second I thought I ought to join
in and look the same, but Harry and I had just finished
writing what we thought was a brilliant script about two
married writers who have been separated but have to
come together to write a film because they have run out
of not just love – but money.

'You and Harry are coming to dinner tonight,' my
mother stated. I tried to look unsurprised.

'Yes, of course,' I said, feebly, and for no reason I
could think of I felt as though I was going to have to take
my driving test again.

Harry and I had not been in favour with my father
lately. *The Happy Communist* had lowered our popularity
rating at Dingley Dell, at least for a bit. Even though my
father had been told that the picture was now called *Sexy
Aliens*, and there were no communists in it, he had still
taken umbrage in the way that only he could. I thought
it vaguely unreasonable.

'The dinner tonight is not for enjoyment,' my mother went on. 'It is for security reasons.'

The palms of my hands became rather warmer than is considered quite nice, and I cleared my throat several times, which I always did when I felt I was sailing into troubled territory at Dingley Dell.

'It seems,' my mother went on, 'that you can be of use to your father, you and er – Harry.'

Since the news that we had written a comedy called *The Happy Communist* everyone at Dingley Dell now referred to Harry as 'er – Harry', as if by not quite remembering his name he would somehow disappear out of my life.

When I told 'er – Harry' that we would be required at dinner, he looked appalled.

'We can't be of any use to your father, we are useless.'

'MI5 like useless people. They use them all the time.'

'But dinner? I mean we were meant to be finishing Act Two, and doing the rewrite on Act One, and I was going to make you Dermot's recipe for stuffed cabbage.'

'It might be nice at Dingley Dell. I mean dinner is often good there. Filet mignon and home-made ice cream—'

'Not your mother's ice cream?'

'No, Mrs Graham's ice cream. You know, the crunchy one you like.'

That did it. Harry would walk on hot coals for Mrs Graham's crunchy ice cream.

My father was a stickler for punctuality. If anyone was late, it would be taken very badly. Five minutes late was a crime.

'Mrs Graham, you know,' he would say. 'She has to get home for Mr Graham, to clean out their canaries and so on. Don't want to make things awkward for her.'

For this reason Harry and I found ourselves, as usual, hanging about in the dustbin area too early in order that we should be absolutely on time. After which we would present ourselves at the front door, looking and feeling pleased.

Which was not how the rest of the assembled company were looking as we went into the drawing room. To say the least, the atmosphere was leaden. Melville, playing the piano, looked as if he was playing it on a sinking ship.

My father gave Harry a penetrating look before pouring him a very large drink. He gave me a very large drink too, which I hugged to me before hiding it under a nearby chair.

'Go on in, Lottie, I'm not joining you tonight. The dinner is only for you and Harry and Hal and Melville – security business,' my mother announced, coming back into the drawing room, retrieving the drink and sitting down with it to listen to the wireless. 'The less people know about this matter the better,' she added.

In the dining room, I sat down with the rest of them, and before long my father started to speak – always stopping when Mrs Graham was in the room. As he spoke I had the distinct feeling Harry and I were in a play someone else had written; not a Trevor Duncan play, I hasten to add, but someone who was keen on skulduggery at the highest level.

It seemed that the famous Shakespearean actor Roland Andrews – always referred to by Hal and Melville as 'dear old Roly' – was about to walk into a sinister plot, which would finish his career and cast a dark shadow over the whole English acting profession. Hollywood would shun our brilliant actors and directors and writers – any taint of communism, socialism, or other isms. In other words, it would be death to all future hopes for film investment in this country.

'Roly is a duck, actually,' Melville stated as the conversation turned to the nature of Roland Andrews' character, 'but he is also gormless. Reality went years ago from playing dear Shakespeare's greatest roles. He is most famous for King Lear, but then there is the Scottish play of course – that split up him and Melinda. They ignored the golden rule, which is never, ever play the starring roles in the Scottish play if you are married. And then of course there's Romeo – he still does Romeo, bless him, although nowadays only on tour, and then only north of Crewe.'

I tried to clear my throat a little too loudly because I could see that Harry was about to make a statement, or worse – ask a question.

'I am wondering, sir,' he asked my father during a pause in the conversation, 'how you all think that Lottie and I can help prevent this sinister plot?'

'Easy, my dear fellow. You have to infiltrate Roly's household, and somehow provide us with the information we need to stop him bringing the house of theatrical cards down around his ears. Roly could end up in jug if he goes on getting involved in something he does not understand. He is not only a well-meaning old monster, but a bit of a dancing bear too.'

'The whole establishment will stand shoulder to shoulder against him,' Melville said in a quiet voice. 'People are still very sensitive on these issues.'

I frowned. This was all getting beyond me, but not it seemed beyond Harry.

'So,' he said. 'You want to use Lottie and myself to – to infiltrate Roland Andrews' household, and somehow rescue him from these sinister plotting communist-leaning characters?'

My father smiled for the first time. 'That's the ticket,' he said.

'You will do splendidly,' Hal announced. 'Young, enthusiastic ... you will have him tied to your cause rather than these other ghastlies, in a few seconds. Besides he's with my agent, couldn't be simpler. I believe you have the perfect script — only just finished, Lottie tells me — ready to wave before him,' he concluded, firmly.

After dinner ended Harry tried to walk home in a normal fashion, but it was just not possible. He kept stopping and having to take deep breaths. I knew this was because he had just agreed to do something neither of us wanted to do.

'I expect you wish you had never had anything to do with me?' I prompted him.

'I do not wish anything like that, I just wish we had said no, but with those three round a table it is impossible to say anything but yes. They are so persuasive. I mean who can refuse to rescue a poor ageing old actor from his enemies? But to have to offer him our script as well, that is true patriotism.'

'It means I will have to take another bit of leave, but apparently that will be made all right with Commander Steerforth, the powers that be will smooth it all over.'

'It means we will have to finish this rewrite on the script, so that they can get it round to him through his agent, which he just so happens to share with Hal.'

'Time for cold towels around the head—'

'And some. It might have helped if you hadn't said we had finished it already.'

Harry stopped walking, or rather wobbling, down the street towards his flat, and faced me.

'I am not changing a word of it, you understand, not even for your father, MI5, MI6 or Uncle Tom Cobley.'

'Why would we have to?' I asked, and it was my turn to gulp for air. 'I mean our script is just going to be a foot in the door.'

'Let's hope he hates it,' Harry said gloomily. 'Of course, there's a good chance he will hate it.'

'Let us pray hard to the God of scripts—'

'Amen to that.'

I don't think we could have prayed hard enough because within a couple of weeks Harry had the call from Hal's agent. At the end of the call Harry put down the telephone with an expression of despair.

'Oh, Lord, he loves it. Apparently we must go round – Tuesday of next week. Make plans at once, free us for this great patriotic task.'

After that Harry had to go for a walk, and he let me go with him.

'It just doesn't feel right,' he moaned, 'sneaking about some poor old star's house on the pretence that we are going to be doing this film together. It just doesn't seem right. I mean the part of the father is hardly huge, is it?'

I agreed the part of the father was not huge, but obviously it was big enough to attract Roland Andrews or we would not be going round, would we?

*

Roland Andrews lived in a very smart part of Chelsea, not quite Belgravia, but very up and coming, and yet enough of the whiff of bohemia to give it a pleasantly raffish air – the front door black and shiny, the brass knocker depicting the twin faces of comedy and tragedy, and the door opened by a butler in a striped apron with a very purposeful feather duster under his arm.

'You are?' he asked in a measured way, with a distinct theatrical timbre.

'That voice has been on many long tours,' I muttered to Harry as the butler left us in the first-floor drawing room.

It was a room filled with the kind of art that makes you feel at home – well, that makes me feel at home. I never quite like a room that has no real paintings on the walls, and this one had a nice collection – not Old Masters but English Impressionists, a Rex Whistler drawing, and a pair of paintings that I could treasure of golden wheat fields, England in the autumn. Above the chimneypiece was a large portrait of Roland Andrews – as Romeo.

At last the door opened and the great man appeared.

Roland Andrews was still slim, but his hair was thinning, and his skin had that slight flush that in late middle age speaks of many enjoyable evenings at the Garrick Club.

'My dear scribes,' he said, warmly, shaking our hands. 'How very pleasant, and bless you for coming.'

Harry and I nodded, still standing.

'It is a great privilege to meet you, sir,' Harry said, filling in the ensuing pause.

I looked at Harry. He wasn't usually so awestruck, and then I remembered that he had been at the first night of the never-to-be-forgotten Roland Andrews' King Lear – a performance so brilliant it was still talked about in lowered tones.

'Sit, please sit.' Roland Andrews indicated some sofas. We sat down obediently as he ensconced himself in a large library chair from which vantage point he could gaze down on us lowly writers.

'I love your script,' he said, smiling. 'I really love it. I read it in one sitting, which is unusual for me. I am so flattered that you thought of sending it to me. I love Mike. I love his attitude, I love the way he puts Sophie down, and yet he is still in love with her, obviously. It is a part made for me.'

He rose from his chair and started to walk about as he spoke, and it was just as well he did as the expression on Harry's face, let alone my own, could only have been described as aghast. Mike, the male lead, was a randy thirty year old.

'I have already thought of how to play him, beginning with the feet of course. One must always start with the feet. Even with Lear I started with the feet.'

'Mr Andrews, sir——' Harry began, but sensing danger I interrupted him before he could get any further.

'How do you see Mike's background, sir?'

There was a pregnant pause, well – all right – just a pause as I made my special silent 'shut up' gesture to Harry, finger-waggling, usually behind my back, but as I was sitting on a lowly sofa for lesser folk, I had to do it in front of me.

By now Harry, pale to the lips, sat in a frozen pose, staring ahead of him as a starving man might who has just had a plate of crumpets pass under his nose only for them to be offered to someone else. I could see that he simply could not believe what he was hearing.

Roland turned from the window where he had been gazing into the street below and gave us his thoughts.

'Oh, I think Mike is the son of a landlady running theatrical digs, don't you?'

Needless to say, I knew Roland Andrews' mother was just such a woman. Harry was about to correct this and tell the great star that actually our fictional Mike was the son of a famous athlete, a father figure whom – as it happened – he greatly resented, when I made my 'shut up' gesture again.

'I wish you would stop doing that,' Harry moaned as Roland Andrews left us to take a telephone call in the next room.

'Just let it happen,' I instructed him. 'Let things unravel … they will have to, I mean no one is going to believe that he can play Mike. It won't happen, just can't.'

'In that case what on earth are we doing here?'

'We're trying to find the wretched compromising document he is being persuaded to sign, remember?'

Harry looked round the immaculately tidy room.

'No point in looking here, there's nowhere to hide it.'

'I don't know.'

I always believe in improving the shining hour, so I immediately struggled up from our sofa and started to look under the cushions. Nothing revealed itself until I dared to raise the seat of the library chair, and lo, before our astonished eyes, and they were astonished, lay a large white envelope.

'Leave it!'

'No, must look. Just must.'

'Drat. Bank statements. Double, double drat. Funny place to keep them.'

There was the sound of someone at the door; Harry flew to it as I shoved the envelope back under the resident cushion.

The someone at the door was the butler. 'So sorry, must fly to the bathroom ...'

'To the left, sir. No, your left, not mine.'

Harry's dash for the little boys' room was enough to distract the butler, who was a person of lofty height. This gave me enough time to sink back down on to our sofa of humble dimensions.

'Sir will be with you in a moment,' the butler told me. 'He has to sign a few documents. People are always after him for his signature, and he is much in demand for so many causes.'

We took the bus home in a state of great relief, because it was now quite obvious to us that we had arrived too late in Roland Andrews' life to be able to prevent him from signing things.

It was a relief, I tell you, to go to bed that night thinking that we would not have to struggle with the worthy old Shakespearean actor impersonating our Mike.

Relief came too soon, as it always seems to with writers.

I was back in the War Office the next day, taking up the reins again, when the telephone rang and it was Harry calling.

'It's still on, the job is still on.'

The arrangement had been that Harry should report back to my father about Andrews, which he had indeed done.

'What do you mean, the job is still on?'

'What do you think I mean? We're to go round there tomorrow morning. Tell you more when I see you.'

Commander Steerforth was impressed.

'Still on active service, eh? Well done. But remember, always make sure of your exit before you go in. It's the golden rule. Can get you out of a lot of trouble, particularly in the Bight.'

I was getting a bit fed up of golden rules, but nevertheless I smiled my thanks, and the day finished with a mound of typing and any number of carbon copies, all of which seemed intent on turning my fingers blue, which was probably better than turning the air blue, which I felt like doing at the very idea of having to go back into the fray with Roland Andrews.

'He's got such a big bottom,' I moaned the following day on the bus to Chelsea.

'Never mind his bottom, it's his face we have to worry about. No amount of make-up will hide those crags and sags.'

Harry stared out of the window and I could feel him wishing that the film he had done had been released, and then wondering if it ever would be.

'I am sorry about all this skulduggery, Harry, but it might lead to real work, mightn't it?'

'Sure, and it might lead to this poor old thespian being put in prison.'

'No, no, they won't do that; they'll do something much worse.'

'Which is?'

'Skew any prospect of his knighthood.'

'Poor old ham. After all that trolling the Bard through the provinces during the war with bombs dropping into his make-up, they would sabotage the ultimate reward?'

'Worse than that – they will ruin his reputation, forever. You know how stuffy people are – any hint of something they don't agree with themselves and, heigh-ho, off you go to the Gulag.'

'That could be quite a smart address – Gulag 1.'

'It might well turn out to be one we will be putting to our writing paper if we don't find this wretched petition he is about to put his paw print on. Myself, I think it's the butler who is influencing him.'

'How do you mean?'

'Well, it is a golden rule in plays and things, when in doubt, make it the maid or the butler. After all, it could easily be the butler hiding the bank statements under the cushion—'

'You think like that and you haven't even acted in repertory theatre, madam?'

'Seen a lot of tatty tours, Clever Drawers.'

After these exchanges we had finally arrived outside the great man's house.

As soon as the front door opened and I re-appraised the butler in his entirety standing in the doorway, I real-ised I might be on to something.

There was something not quite right about him. I don't just mean that I could see he was wearing ladies' nylons, and not socks with his shoes – after all, it was a theatrical household – but because he had a shifty look to his nostrils. People always go on about a shifty look to the eyes, but nostrils give away a great deal. They can open and close too quickly, as this chap's nostrils were doing just that, as if he was a horse coming off the gallops. It was not natural; at least I didn't think it was.

'He keeps looking down at us as if we smell,' Harry whispered after the butler had shown us to our sofa and closed the drawing-room door behind us.

'So you noticed that too? I think it most suspicious. I think he thinks we are most suspicious. Perhaps he knows we are not here just for the script, perhaps he knows that Roland Andrews is making a tit of himself thinking he can play Mike?'

'Or he knows we are from Another Source?'

'Hardly— '

'He might be from Another Source himself.'

This was getting trying. I really hated the whole double-agent thing — I mean who was who and why was fine, but as soon as an agent was playing both ends against the middle, then no one knew where they really were, and not likely to find out either, so I was very relieved when the door opened again and this time it was not the nostril-inflating butler, but the star himself.

'My favourite twosome!'

He looked so pleased to see us that I felt quite awful to think we were busy leading him on, and I could see that Harry did too. There was such genuine warmth in Andrews' eyes, and — after we had struggled to our feet — his handshake seemed so sincere that I just wanted to go home and call the whole thing off.

'I have read and re-read your piece—'

I frowned. I wasn't sure I wanted our writing described in this way – property, yes, but piece seemed a bit fragmentary for my large ego – unless it was preceded by 'master', of course, following which I would give a modest smile and nudge Harry to do the same.

'So, to continue. I have read and re-read the piece—'

There was a small pause as I noticed Harry now openly wincing at the repetition of the word 'piece'.

'Yes,' the great man continued. 'And I have come to the conclusion that the principal parts are perfect for me and for Dame Nellie, but the father needs to be older than you have made him, don't you think?'

We both saw at once what he was getting at. By making the father much older, he and Dame Nellie would look as young as new-born kittens.

We were totally silenced, which was unusual.

'I expect you cannot believe your luck at the idea that Dame Nellie would, could or has even contemplated doing your film, but the truth is she has, and we would be reprising our great partnership in *Love on the Move*. Who can forget our scene – so beautifully written by Sir Paul – in the Morris Minor on Beachy Head? Do you know, people still come up to us and say they are convinced, however many times they see the film, that we are going to release the brake and depart this world together.'

I tried hard not to remember my mother telling me she had seen *Love on the Move* in France and the cinema audience rocked with laughter from start to finish, but then as she always said the French take love more lightly.

'I am sure we can age the father,' I said quickly, before Harry could say something quite different.

'I thought perhaps he could be in a wheelchair?'

'With the best will in the world, I don't think he can surprise Mike with how fit he still is from a wheelchair.'

'He could have very, very strong – hands.'

'I am sorry, sir, but I think that would skew the story too much. We will age him, of course, but no wheelchair.'

The star looked surprised at Harry's firm tone while I stared past him and wondered if we would ever get to see the stupid document of a political nature Roland Andrews was meant to be signing.

'White hair then, very white hair ... we'll put that into the script.'

I didn't like the word 'we', but I let it pass as Harry was beginning to look irritated and not bothering to conceal it.

'I was thinking that Sir John would be perfect for the father, but whether he will do it is another thing. He is terribly vain about his age, you know. Just can't see what has happened to him.'

At this Roland Andrews ran his fingers lightly through the sides of his own deeply black hair.

'You must be thrilled at the idea of Dame Nellie and myself, are you not?'

We nodded dumbly, two birds on a wire.

'There is only one fly in the ointment at the moment.' We both stared up at our star, both feeling as if we had just swallowed one.

'Darling Nellie is left of centre – always has been – and she wants me to sign this document supporting one of her most treasured political causes. It is a terrible dilemma for me. I respect her feelings, but not this document. However, for the sake of the film—'

'Don't do it, sir!' Harry struggled to his feet. I followed, albeit more slowly. 'Nothing is worth sacrificing your political conscience for, for – for which to sacrifice your political conscience.'

'No,' I agreed quickly, thinking of my father and his grim expression over dinner. 'But for the sake of the film—'

'Don't sign, sir,' Harry went on, holding him, lightly, by both arms. 'Think of everything you did in the war, all the bombs dropping as you played Romeo, and Lear, and … and all those.' He looked up with assumed reverence at the portrait above the chimneypiece. 'Think, think, think!'

I thought there were at least two too many 'thinks' at this point, but Roland Andrews did not appear to agree.

His eyes filled with tears.

'I did not think that your generation would ever appreciate what we did. This is the first time that someone your age has even mentioned what we thespians went through on those tours. I mean Crewe alone—'

'Crewe, exactly! Think of Crewe.'

Roland walked away down the room, looking thoughtful.

'Ghastly as it is, I think you are right. If Nellie sticks to her stance over me signing, I can't. I shan't sign!' He started to walk back up the elegant room. 'After all, it is I to whom you came, not Nellie. It is I who was asked to shoulder the film, not Nellie.'

He paused then and, bending down, lifted the cushion under which we knew the envelope with the bank statements lay fermenting.

'I do wish Shaughnessy would stop putting my bank statements under cushions, really I do. It's a habit from the war, you know, he thinks it plumps them up more and saves on feathers.' He took out the contents of the envelope and glanced at them briefly. 'These are from nineteen thirty-nine ... gracious how times change. Look at the cost of the telephone then!' He threw the papers on the fire. 'So, now we have come to a decision, have we not?'

Neither Harry nor I realised that we had, but we did our best to look as if we had – I opted for grave but responsible. I didn't look at Harry, but I think his expression might have had a touch of muted triumph.

There was a profound silence, which I would soon recognise as being that of a star thinking, but I was at that point unversed in their ways.

'So, no Nellie, no signing of the petition, so whom to ask now?'

We knew enough to keep our traps shut.

'I shall ask Dickie to ask Julia Mannering. She is so easy to work with. We did the factories together during the war, singing and doing sketches during their lunch hours. They hated us, but it kept their spirits up throwing spent cartridges at us. Yes, Julia and I will fit the bill all right. And Shaughnessy will be thrilled. He loves her dearly, they are always gossiping on the blower of a morning when I'm sleeping in. Yes, Julia would be perfect, and not so young that we wouldn't believe in her love for me, and then – the parting, and the coming together in this Beatrice and Benedict of a partnership. It could be glorious, your words and our acting, our energy – all quite perfect. We shall have a hit! And to celebrate—'

He rang the bell for Shaughnessy.

'Bring in the wretched petition, Shawn ducky.'

'Very well, sir.'

Moments later we watched with huge satisfaction as the petition joined the bank statements, and Shaughnessy left, smiling so widely that we knew at once he had been listening at the door.

For a second Roland Andrews watched him leaving with an affectionate but despairing expression on his face.

'I'm sorry about Shawn,' he said, dropping his voice. 'I keep telling him about the ladders in his nylons, but he doesn't listen.'

Harry looked sympathetic.

'My mother always says soap can stop ladders,' he told Roland.

Roland nodded, but I could see that he wanted us to go so he could telephone his agent to telephone Julia Mannering's agent, and put the wheels of casting into motion.

*

As we went back on the bus I realised that we should be feeling triumphant. After all we had achieved our objective, we had done our patriotic duty, Roland Andrews would still be in line for a knighthood, and his butler might even stop the ladders in his stockings happening. I had no idea which was the most important to whom, but I knew that my father, and indeed my mother for completely different reasons, would be very pleased.

Such was not the case with Harry, however.

For the next few days whenever we met to work at his flat he was in a blue funk.

'All these old birds staring into each other's eyes, our film is ruined,' he said, again and again, until finally I met him for work wearing a pixie hood.

'Please take that thing off, it does nothing for you.'

I lifted one of the pixie's ears.

'Not until you take off the LP – moan, moan, moan. We should be getting on with something else. Forget *Making the Play*. Okay, we loved writing it, and we loved writing *The Happy Communist* – and look what happened to that. We'll get paid. We'll get a credit. That, as they say, is show business.'

'Have you seen Julia Mannering lately? My mother saw her in Peter Jones' haberdashery department. Said she looked older than God.'

'And my mother said the British love old dolls and guys. Prefer them actually, and that great writer Somerset Maugham said the English would never go and see a ballerina dance unless they knew she had only one leg, or an actress unless they were in agony that she was going to forget all her words. It stirs them up, makes them love performers more. They will love Roland Andrews and Julia Mannering. You'll see. Now where's the next idea?'

Harry looked sulky.

'As a matter of fact, I did have one this morning.'

We sat down opposite each other, and before long he had quite forgotten about *Making the Play* as we started to map out a comedy about two young writers, an old actor and a butler, only this time the document under the cushion was the wretched petition, which Harry said added edge. I was only too happy to agree, even though I thought he was wrong.

As to my father, he was muted in his appreciation of our work, as he would be.

'Good stuff,' he said, patting Harry on the shoulder, lightly.

He knew this was big coming from my father, so he smiled broadly, and accepted a stiff drink. I had a better time with Commander Steerforth.

'Come off active service and won the battle too. Well done!' he said, smiling happily. 'Now any chance of a slice of Victoria sponge from the canteen, do you think?'

I beetled off to get the Commander early tea and am sorry to say that the moment his face lit up at the sight of the lovely fresh slice of sponge meant more to me than the sight of that wretched petition burning in Roland Andrews' fireplace.

But then Harry always suspected that I was deeply shallow, and I am sorry to say that I think he might have been right.

THE CONVERSION

Television was not something that anyone ever discussed in our house. To put it another way, it was not a word that was mentioned, or even referred to as existing. Dingley Dell was not alone in this. I myself knew no one who had a television. To a person, everyone's parents had all disapproved of the young queen allowing her Coronation to be filmed by the BBC.

Of course, they had not seen the ceremony in their own homes – that would have been tantamount to being found to be a card-carrying member of the Communist Party. If questioned on the subject they had only ever seen the film of the Coronation in their clubs, or in the basement on Nanny's set. It was just not done to own up to having a television set.

My father seemed completely unaware of this self-imposed embargo among nice people. He loved television. He thought it was the best thing since sliced bread, which he also loved – either fried with his early-morning breakfast bacon and egg, or done up in a nice squishy sardine sandwich.

One of his most engaging characteristics was that he simply did not understand snobbery of any kind. Of course, due to running agents and often as not working until the early hours, he did not have much time to actually watch television, so he particularly enjoyed it on a Sunday evening when he would sit silently fascinated by a conjuror, or a chap putting contestants through a series of simple word games on a magnetic board.

'I enjoy this,' he would murmur if you came across him in the back room where the small Bush television was discreetly housed. 'They win quite a lot of money at this game, you know – quite a lot – and if they don't they still get a prize. Jolly good stuff.'

My mother was tolerant of his affection for television, but she was also insistent that he did not mention anything that he had seen there at the lunch or dinner table. The reason for this was not that she felt embarrassed by it, but because it raised panic among actors, particularly Hal and Melville who even when out of work, or resting as they called it, would sigh and shake their heads at this new medium.

Harry understood their reluctance even to talk about it.

'It's because it's live,' he said with some authority. 'It scares the poo-bah out of them. I mean if you dry in the theatre – the words go and you can't think of the next phrase, let alone sometimes why you're there – and fear does do that to you, you're doing it not in front of an audience of a few hundred in television, it's in front of millions.'

'In fact, Hal told me that Melville was offered a great big television role as a police officer and turned it down. He wouldn't even go near it, because he was so frightened of what would happen to his career if he flopped. I mean apparently you are sunk, but sunk, if you don't bring it off whereas in the theatre there is always the next night to get it right.'

'Or not,' said Harry shortly. 'They're just funks.'

'They do great radio roles, they don't mind those. Hal was brilliant the other night as a Nazi commander.'

'Type casting,' Harry said, even more shortly.

'And Melville played Feste so beautifully last Christmas—'

'Feste is one of those parts – like the waiter in Shaw's *You Never Can Tell* – where you always walk off with the notices.'

I was about to continue but stopped. After all it was not my subject. I had never acted. Besides, Harry was in a restless mood. I could tell that because he had taken to doing headstands against his sitting-room wall. I knew him well enough to know that to go on talking to him when he was upside down made him irritable, so I left him and went back to Dingley Dell.

*

At MI5 the next day Arabella gave me one of her sphinx-like looks. 'Trouble at mill?' she asked over a coffee in the canteen.

'Harry is very restless. We haven't written a word of the new script for days. Every time I go round to the flat to start work he diverts me in some way. I feel like an artistic wallflower.'

'When a man is restless, my mother says, it is always either because they are having an affair or they're bored with you, which really amounts to the same thing.'

I couldn't imagine anyone getting bored of Arabella's beautiful mother. Quite apart from being beautiful she had been a famous agent in the war, working for Special Operations Executive in Europe; she was also famed for her ability to entrance men. Some of them had never got over her, at least two taking Holy Orders rather than settle for anyone else. Currently she was enjoying a warm friendship with Commander Steerforth, a widower of many years' standing, but very shy. Apparently shyness in men was always indicated by how many flowers they bought you. It seemed that Commander Steerforth was never without a bunch of beautiful blooms.

'Monty loves flowers but these vast arrangements are nutty nuts,' Arabella told me factually.

'Running out of vases, is he?'

'Just that – every day a positive herbaceous border. But no one has the heart to stop the Commander, bless him.'

I never like the conversation turning away from me for very long, so I brought it back to where I thought it should be.

'So you think Harry's having an affair?'

'No, precious bane, I do not think that. I just said what my mother would say. Even so ...' Arabella's gaze was obscured by a drift of cigarette smoke. It was a habit of hers when she'd had enough of my egoism. 'Even so,' she said after a moment, 'there must be something wrong for Harry not to want to be working with you.' She lowered her gaze. 'You don't think that Dermot has poached him as a writing partner, do you?'

I gasped, but only inwardly. 'That would be infidelity indeed.'

I was determined to put on a brave face at the suggestion, but my insides had turned to ice. Harry and I had always agreed that artistic infidelity would be far, far worse than any other kind. We were both convinced that writing with someone was far more intimate than making love.

'It's a possibility,' Arabella continued relentlessly, reluctant to give up on her disturbing theory. 'I mean what with both of them out of work and resting, there must be a lot of talk at the flat.'

'They did make another stuffed cabbage together the other night—'

'You didn't eat any of it, did you?'

'Of course not.'

'Some of those Bolshevik recipes can be fatal. My mother told me that behind the Iron Curtain they can put razor blades in stuffed cabbage and no one ever notices until the pudding.'

I went home on the number nine bus, and began thinking, which I always find a trial, but Arabella had given me food for thought, or rather food poisoning for thought.

Forget Iago and his stupid hankie, what about Dermot and his recipes?

Harry always said men usually preferred each other's company at work because they could say and do things that they would not do or say if there were a female person, not their mother, present. How to approach the subject?

The following evening, after work, I decided to join Harry at the headstand wall where he was practising some kind of oriental thinking.

'Harry?' I said from upside down, which was not easy for me.

'Yes.'

'Did you enjoy Dermot's cabbage the other night?'

'Please, Lottie, I was just beginning to feel better.'

That brought me down from the wall. I settled for cross-legged on the floor and watched Harry intently, because I thought I might be able to detect from his back view if he was lying.

'Harry — be honest — are you unhappy with the idea we are working on?'

He joined me on the floor.

'I do have a problem, but that is not it,' he confessed.

He gave me a deep look and I waited, braced for the news that he had committed artistic adultery with Dermot.

'I have been offered a big part on television — a play, a long play — and I can't make up my mind whether or not to do it. Gus, would you believe, is dead against it, says it will finish me for films. Almost as bad as acting in a commercial, he says.'

We both laughed. An actor appearing in a commercial was such a funny idea. Appear in an advertisement and after that you had no one but the cheque for a friend.

'The thing is it's not just a play, and a very long play, but it is for — ITV.'

Suddenly it all fell into place. Harry's quandary had affected his appetite for writing for good reason; I could see the problem straight away. If he took the part he would have money in his pocket, and if he didn't — well, it was back to Dermot and his Bolshevik recipes, and costly games of squash with Gus. Nothing would change. There was a time limit to enjoying bohemian poverty and perhaps Harry had reached that limit. He had even had to sell his watch a while back, admittedly to me — but even so.

'I think you should do it, Harry.'

He stared at me.

'That didn't take long.'

'Well, you've done a film, so no one can say you haven't been offered one before and stop offering them to you now, and you haven't been offered anything else, so why not? After all you'll be doing a big role and be seen, which is lots better than not being seen — as Melville always says.'

Harry kissed me, briefly, which he always did when he was not really thinking about kissing but just thinking, something he did better than myself on account of having been given a different sort of education, which unlike mine didn't insist on flower arranging and how to get out of a taxi without showing your petticoat.

'What I like about you, Lottie, can be summed up in one word.'

I waited, but Harry always needed a gasper after a headstand, so off he went in search of one of Dermot's ciggies.

He came back smoking.

'I shall do as you say and do it now. I will tell Gus, yes, I will.' He picked up the telephone receiver. And then he replaced it.

'Are you rehearsing telephone acting?' I asked in a kindly voice.

'Yes, I am.'

Harry breathed out Gauloise smoke in a very impressive manner. 'But I am also trying to stay calm.'

He sat down suddenly.

'Gus will have a twin fit,' he announced, rather too loudly as if we were standing on a station platform.

'You employ Gus – he doesn't employ you.'

'There speaks an innocent bystander.'

Harry gave me a bitter look and I felt duly crushed.

'Agents run this business, Lottie. I am lucky to have one at all. They can get rid of you, you know – just like that.' He snapped his fingers. 'And try getting work without an agent.' He snorted, lightly inhaled his Gauloise and started coughing. 'I think,' he said finally, 'I will go and see Gus rather than – rather than do it on the phone.'

*

Back at the coal face at MI5 and struggling with six sheets of carbon paper that were refusing to wind themselves anywhere except round my fingers, I was in a frosty mood.

'You look as if you might need a thrilling piece of Victoria sponge,' Arabella announced with her usual authority.

I agreed and we retired yet again to the canteen.

'Any more of these tea breaks and communism will take a hold of this country,' the lady behind the serving counter said, slicing the Victoria sponge.

'Our people are at a conference,' Arabella explained, looking dignified.

'Oh, well, that's all right then. Why not ask Stalin in and give him some Victoria sponge? And a cup of tea too while you're at it.'

'She's such a spy,' Arabella said as we sat down with our backs to her.

'Well, she would be, wouldn't she?' I said, sounding suddenly reasonable. Arabella thought for a minute.

'I wonder whether they run checks on people in catering.'

Frankly I couldn't have cared, but Arabella was more dutiful than I so she went on pondering the subject of catering people being double agents, while I moaned on about Harry and his indecision. About his acting part on ITV and his agent being against it, and my being for it, until Arabella finished her sponge and put down her new personalised cake fork that she kept in her handbag, and gave a very loud sigh.

'There is a Cold War on, atom bombs being made on every street corner, and the whole of Europe could be swamped by Russians intent on exterminating us. Please forgive me if I could care less about Harry appearing on ITV.'

I stared at her in admiration. Arabella had a way with her, there was no doubt about it.

Later at Harry's flat, while the smell of yet more cabbage being cooked assailed me from all sides – did Dermot eat nothing else? – I repeated Arabella's speech. I could say *to* Harry, but really, if I am honest, it was *at* Harry.

He stared at me, hurt and reproach in both eyes. Well, now I think about it, it would be quite difficult to confine reproach to one eye.

'I know you are speaking the truth, Lottie, but that is not your truth. You are far too nice to suggest that my being on ITV does not matter as much as the Bomb.'

I said nothing because actually I wasn't that nice, and we both knew it. A whole minute went by during which I thought I too might take up smoking Gauloise cigarettes.

'Very well, I will do the part, but only because you think it is right.'

'Oh, thanks. So now your career will be in ruins because of me,' I said, bitterly, but Harry did not hear the bitter bit – he was already dialling his agent and sounding stern with the telephonist, insisting on being put through, and thereafter followed a conversation to which I was not party because I was in what Elizabethans called the privy, but which my father for some reason called 'the aunt'. My mother, however, always determined to be polite, called it the 'excuse me'. I on the other hand called it the la-la. One way or another it went to show how reticent the English were about loos and toilets, although why I could not say without going for a further education course, something which I have always avoided on the sound premise that too much thinking can make you weak.

When I finished doing my hair in the bathroom, staring into the cracked pub mirror with its *Say Seager's Gin* slogan, I emerged to the unfamiliar sight of Harry smiling for the first time in days.

'You won't believe this,' he said, 'Gus only thinks it is a good idea. I mean after all this. He is starting negotiations this very minute. Just think, Lottie, I will be on the dreaded telly for the first time, and you and your parents will be able to watch me.'

After Harry kissed me I gave a crooked smile. Unfortunately he spotted it.

'What now?'

'Nothing.'

'It's never nothing when you give the crooked smile. What?'

'We don't have ITV. We have never been converted.'

'In that case it's time you were. Not to have ITV looks like prejudice.'

'My mother didn't like the idea of commercials.'

'Here we go again.'

'I actually like them. I saw some on Monty's television in his sitting room. I saw a woman pour coffee out of a jug on to a white shirt—'

'Lottie. Stick to the subject. Look, I know a chap who can go round to Dingley Dell and convert your parents' set. He's called Len. He's a good man.'

'I'll have to ask my mother. And she'll have to ask my father. And they will have to keep it from Hal and Melville.'

But Harry was not listening; he had picked up his script and was walking up and down and learning lines in a muttering kind of way. I left him for our favourite coffee bar and some deep thinking before confronting my mother on the issue of conversion.

'You think we should convert?'

'Well, it might be fun. Harry is going to be on in a few weeks, and my feeling is that you might enjoy it.'

'I'll have to ask your father, I don't think he knows about ITV.'

The matter was not referred to for some time, until eventually even Harry thought there might be something up.

'Perhaps MI5 don't like commercials?'

'They should do – personally, I think they'll bring down the Iron Curtain.'

My father and I had long disagreed on this. He could not see that heavenly white washing could brainwash people in a good way.

Finally I was called into my father's study to face an interrogation. 'Your mother tells me you think we should convert?'

'You might enjoy it,' I said, feebly.

'Indeed we might,' he agreed. 'And this fellow Len, this friend of er – Harry, he can do the conversion?'

I said that was the rumour, although I did not know Len personally.

'Your mother insists we will have to keep this matter between ourselves. Hal and Melville are a bit sensitive about television and so on, they imagine it will destroy theatre. They think everyone will sit at home and watch it and not want to go out.'

My thoughts were racing. Hal and Melville were around the house a great deal at the moment, as they would be on account of suffering a great many setbacks. How was I to get Len in and out to the back room without them noticing?

'I'll tell him to disguise himself,' Harry suggested, cheerfully.

'What as?'

'I don't know – a plumber, or something?'

Of course, inevitably, Len arrived just as Hal was leaving the house. 'There's someone at the front door who says he's a plumber, Lottie,' he boomed, before frowning at Len. 'You're dressed very smartly for a plumber, aren't you?' he added accusingly.

Len looked towards me with the expression of a drowning man waiting to be thrown a rope.

'I once played a plumber in rep. I even took care to smell like one,' Hal went on progressing past Len, 'and I certainly did not costume him like that.'

'He's got a change in his bag, haven't you, Len?' I asked hastily. 'Come with me and we can talk about taps.'

We closeted ourselves in the back room.

'I'm sorry about that, but what could I do? Harry told me to say I was a plumber.'

'Never mind that now, you'd better have a look at the Bush before we go any further. I mean, you know, conversion might not be possible on this.'

I took the Chinese shawl off the Bush telly with something of a flourish, hoping that it would not look as small and old as it normally did.

Len stared at it. The Bush was one of the first models to be produced way back when a radio was still called a wireless. It had been a surprise present to my grandmother from my grandfather, not because she longed for one but because *he* wanted to watch Annette Mills and

Muffin the Mule on whom he doted, but when he died no one else wanted it so my mother took it on out of pity.

Len gave me a deep look.

'I haven't seen one of these in a while, I must say.'

He went on staring at the Bush in deeper and deeper fascination.

'Since the Coronation people have more modern sets. Lots more modern sets ... everywhere I go a new model. This one is going to be a bit of a challenge, and Harry did warn me – but not quite what a challenge.'

I made solicitous noises.

'It might respond to the operation,' Len mused. 'Or it might not. If it doesn't then I'm afraid it might end up deep frozen.'

'What happens then?' I asked nervously, thinking of my father's favourite programme on Sunday evenings.

'Well, a television has to respond to conversion, it can't just convert. It has to want to convert.'

'I don't want the old Bush to be forced to convert, really I don't. I think that would be awful.'

Len nodded to me to move away from the door.

'I hear,' he said, lowering his voice, 'that Harry is not going to be on the BBC but on the Other Side?'

'Just for one play. He has to work, Len.'

'Of course he does, course he does.' Len paused. 'So, do you want to go for the whole conversion, do you want to risk it? Have you faith in me?'

I cleared my throat.

'Yes, Len. Go for the whole conversion. The Bush is strong – it has had to be to last this long with us.'

I left him, but I did not go very far as I had promised my mother I would guard the door while he was operating.

I was hovering outside trying to look personable when Melville passed by.

'Anything wrong, Lottie? You have the look of a stricken rabbit.'

I smiled weakly.

'Just thinking, you know, I do that sometimes.'

Melville frowned.

'If you're thinking perhaps you should sit down?'

I shook my head.

'No, really, if I sit down when I'm thinking I always fall asleep.'

'How irritating.'

'Yes,' I agreed, clearing my throat.

Melville frowned, remembering something.

'I had an uncle like that. He could only think when he was mounted on a horse. Once he got off – his mind went quite blank.'

As I watched Melville going off into the morning I felt bad. What would he and Hal make of us all not just watching a television, but a converted television? They would think much less of us, particularly if they knew that Harry was going to be on it in a very long play.

Len came to the door and silently beckoned to me.

'I think I may have solved it. It has taken some thinking out. These old televisions do not like conversion, they like to stick to what they know, which is the BBC, and really you can't blame them.'

'It's very good of you to try, really. It has hardly ever been watched, you know, only on Sunday evenings when my father does like to tune in to *It's Still Sunday!*'

'We always watch that, as a family. The spelling game on it helps the children, my wife says.'

'You mean when they put up jumbled words?'

'That's the job.' He nodded. 'So now, here we are on Auntie BBC, you agree?'

I nodded appreciatively.

'That's a good picture you've got there, Len.'

'Not bad for an old set. Now, watch.' He pushed a long handle to the side, newly fitted. 'Just one shove – there – still watching? Good, stay watching ... now there! Soap powder advertisement, must be ITV. Now another shove and we are back to Auntie BBC and the potter's wheel. You have a go.'

It took a bit of shoving but I managed, and when my mother returned home later that day, I took her into the back room for a lesson.

'Just watch this.' She stared in admiration, her head on one side. 'Now you have a go.'

She gave a tentative push. 'No, you've got to really shove.'

She soon got the hang of it, after which she wiped her hands with her lace hankie.

'Of course we'll only need the other side if ever er – Harry is on.'

'But it's good to have it anyway.'

'Just must keep it from Hal and Melville. They still don't know about it.' She threw the large Chinese silk shawl over the Bush, and sighed happily. 'Well, I'm glad that's all over; these sorts of things are always such a worry.'

Later I went round to the flat, to find Harry with his script.

'Len's converted Dingley Dell,' I told him happily, taking his script from him to hear his lines. 'He's put in a handle and you just shove it over and ITV comes up.'

But Harry was no longer listening, he was already in the role.

Over the next hour I found myself frowning at what he was saying. The dialogue he was meant to be learning was so convoluted that it didn't seem quite English.

'It's not quite English, Lottie,' he admitted later over a coffee. 'The writer is a foreigner who came to this country before the last war. He has had great reviews for his work, in the *Observer* and the *Scotsman*. The critics like his take on English, especially the Scots – but they don't have to learn it.'

'Just think of the cheque,' I said in an encouraging voice.

'I do, every minute of every hour,' Harry told me, miserably.

At MI5 Arabella appeared fascinated by the telly conversion at Dingley Dell.

'Do you think Len could do it for Monty? Could he convert that set?'

'I'm sure he could. It didn't take him long to do at Dingley Dell.'

'Probably best if you bring Len round yourself, you know how upset Monty can get if he thinks someone who isn't Harrods is coming.'

Len was impressed by the address. It was the first time his van had been parked in SW1.

'Hardly a spit from Harrods' food department,' he said, in a lowered tone, and I noticed that he had changed into a suit with matching hankie and tie out of respect for the grand location.

To my delight Len and Monty took one look at each other and instantly made friends. Monty did not raise his wig, because he wasn't thinking, but he did tuck a bit back from his ear. And Len and I followed him through the kitchen and pantry to his own demesne, a bed-sitting room complete with television.

It was the first time I had been in Monty's part of the flat since he'd moved in to look after Arabella's mother. He had made his bed-sitting room so stylish he could have given tips to a professional designer.

The television was covered by an opera cloak, which he was able to remove with a great flourish.

'Now this won't need a handle,' Len told him, 'this will only need a change of buttons.'

'Could you do your best to match them?'

'It will be a pleasure. This set is one of my favourites.'

Len nodded in the direction of Harrods – which was out of the window and over the rooftops.

'Came from – ahem?'

'They took the window out to bring it in here and install it, so as not to disturb Madam.'

'If you are one of the elite there is nothing Harrods will not do for you.'

Monty attempted to look modest, but not for long because of course Len was only confirming what Monty already knew.

I went outside on to the fire escape while the operation was taking place because I felt I was in the way, and anyway I kept fearing that Monty's telly might not react very well and that made me feel nervy.

The doorbell rang, and I thought to answer it but rejected the idea in case it was Commander Steerforth visiting and he would feel embarrassed at seeing me.

Monty passed me, sighing.

'Please, please, not more blooms,' he muttered, only to return with a large bouquet.

'Sometimes I have even been forced to put them in finger bowls,' he complained, rolling his eyes.

I indicated that I would wait for Len downstairs, and eventually he drove me back to Dingley Dell.

'That's one of the best conversions I've ever done,' he said as he parked outside Dingley Dell at a very unfortunate moment.

'What are you doing in a television van?' Hal boomed at me as I joined him on the top step.

'Len's a friend of Harry's and his friend has a – you know.' I made a box-like gesture.

'Not a very big one,' I added hastily as Hal's nostrils flared.

'Big or small, they are the curse of civilisation.'

I tried to look vague, but must have ended up looking guilty.

'You've never watched, have you?' Hal demanded, throwing his scarf on to a hook.

'Oh, look, Hal, a message from your agent,' I said, quickly holding up a telephone message taken by Mrs Graham.

That put paid to our conversation, or rather Hal's interrogation of me, and I shot upstairs to change before I went round to Harry's flat where nothing was going very well.

'Rehearsals are a nightmare,' he moaned. 'Everyone's drying all over the place.'

'Surely not—'

'They are, they have hardly opened their mouths before they have to shout prompt! In fact, the cast have renamed the play *Prompt*. You should hear them in the canteen, moan, moan, moan; it's replaced "rhubarb" as a crowd noise.'

'Oh, I expect it will be all right.'

But of course it wasn't at all right, and I knew that from the look that Harry gave me.

'I will tell you how un-all right live television is. Last month one of Dermot's friends had a door jam on him – had to make his entrance through Sherlock Holmes' fireplace. He didn't have a covering line so he said "Doorbell wasn't working", and then of course they all went. And he will never work again, poor man.'

Harry was in such a stew I tried not to find this funny.

'Only two days to go and even our famous ex-Hollywood star is looking seedy.'

The night of the play my father and mother had to go out to a cocktail party, but knowing that Harry was on the newly converted Bush telly they duly hurried home to watch him, which I found oddly touching, but my father was like that – he always liked to support his old agents, even ones like Harry who made a bit of a pickle of everything. I was feeling both thrilled and excited until my mother found me something to do.

'You keep guard against Hal or Melville coming by while we warm up the set,' she stated. I hung about the hall feeling, and probably looking, like a spare hairnet. Finally the door opened and my mother beckoned me in.

'Ghastly, too ghastly.'

I went in and saw my father standing looking at Len's handle as if it was a hand grenade.

'It simply won't budge,' my mother said, speaking for him. 'It will only do BBC. I can't understand it, it was fine this morning when I showed Mrs Graham because she wants hers done too.'

We all stood about staring at it forlornly.

'Such a pity,' my mother said, many times. 'We came back from the Ormsbys specially – although we didn't say why, of course.'

I was to meet Harry afterwards. As I hailed a taxi at the appropriate time I was so glad that I had heard his lines. There would be no tripping me up over what the play was about. I almost felt smug. As I walked into the restaurant and went up to the table where Harry was sitting, I was all smiles.

'Marvellous, marvellous, simply marvellous—'

Harry looked at me and I can only describe his expression as tight. 'Before you go any further, Lottie –

the play was cancelled on account of the political crisis.'

It was my turn to have a tight expression.

'That's what I mean – marvellous, marvellous that – it's been cancelled – because, because let's face it, you weren't enjoying doing it.'

Seeing Harry's expression I knew just how Dermot's friend had felt when he shot down the chimney to face Sherlock Holmes. Finally Harry smiled and patted my cheek in a paternal kind of way. 'Well done, Lottie,' he murmured. 'I honestly think you could take over from Houdini when it comes to getting out of tight corners.'

I felt oddly proud, and then I told him about Len's handle getting stuck on BBC, and we had a lovely laugh and dinner and went home and talked about our new idea, which was very close to saying we lived happily ever after, because new ideas make you feel like that.

THE RETURN

I knew something was up when Arabella asked me to lunch at Fenwick's. We hadn't lunched there for a while on account of trying to save up for holidays in faraway places that I always pretended I yearned to go to, when I would far rather be having spaghetti Bolognese in a coffee bar with Harry.

'It's not about Commander Steerforth's flowers and Monty, is it?' I asked, determined on getting down to the nitty and the gritty before I ordered, because being left in ignorance during lunch gives me indigestion.

'Oh, no, we've solved that,' Arabella said, airily. 'Monty takes them all round to the nurses at the local hospital and they put loving notes on them.'

'How do you mean?'

'Some people never get a card or a flower or a visit, so the nurses put "*Thinking of you at this time, from a loving friend*" on Commander Steerforth's flowers, and the lonely patients are delighted. Also it gives them something to think about – you know, who the loving friend might be, and so on – takes their minds off everything.'

I frowned.

'But supposing they don't have any friends?'

'That's the whole point, Lottie. Really, I don't know how Harry stands you.'

'Nor do I,' I agreed, settling on an egg salad with double mayonnaise.

'No, the Commander and my beautiful mother are very well suited. He gives her flowers, takes her to a play, and brings her home. Monty insists on waiting up for her, so of course the Commander dare not keep her out late. It is a very happy arrangement. Nowadays my mother likes to be admired but does not want anyone what she calls "hanging around". She says if she needs that she will get a cat.'

I frowned again. I didn't think that Commander Steerforth would like to be compared to a cat.

'Do you want to get to the point or shall I?' I asked, feeling hungry and impatient at the same time. Arabella instantly assumed her best Gandhi-like expression.

'This is not to be repeated to anyone, but something has happened to Zuzu.'

'Does Zuzu know?'

Arabella closed her eyes very, very slowly and then opened them again – something at which she was very accomplished.

'When things happen to people, Lottie, they are usually the first to know.'

I thought about it for a minute.

'Not everyone,' I said, thinking of myself. 'Sometimes things happen to people and they don't really realise.'

'As soon as you start eating I will tell you.'

Arabella knew me too well. Eating was one of the best times to get me listening.

Arabella on the other hand could eat and talk at the same time because she was very elegant like that.

'Zuzu is in grave trouble with Head of Section because of something. But no one knows quite what.'

'Is she back then?'

'Yes, she's been sent home from Singapore or wherever she was, but no one must tell Monty. He will get too excited.'

I thought Monty was not the only one. I felt very excited at the thought of seeing Zuzu again.

'Is she having visitors?'

'She's not in hospital, Lottie, just in trouble with the powers that be.' Arabella threw me a deep look. I caught it deftly before she continued, 'Do you think your father might help?'

I frowned.

'She's not in his Section.'

'I know she's not in his Section,' Arabella said with commendable restraint, 'but sometimes people in other Sections can help.'

'I'll ask him,' I said, happily going back to my egg mayonnaise.

'What will you ask him?'

'Whatever you want me to,' I said, closing my eyes because I loved mayonnaise and Harry hated it so I always had to have it 'out'– when he was not there – or he felt queasy.

'That's settled then.'

What I found out a little later was that Zuzu was indeed in the claggy. It seemed she had started an affair with an international star who was on location filming near where she worked for MI5 in Singapore. The newspapers were now following the story, hoping against hope that she was going to turn out to be a sort of Mata Hari put in by MI5. I thought it all sounded like a puff of smoke that would soon drift off to the Gulag. But there was more to it than a short piece in a daily newspaper, because the international star had been implicated in a political scandal in America.

'Imagine that.' I sighed with admiration as I heard who the star was. 'It takes Zuzu to have an affair with someone like him.'

For a second I felt vaguely envious, imagining her wafting about in silken robes while the star gazed at her in adoration.

'It takes Zuzu to be that loopy.'

'They can't do anything to her, can they?'

It was Arabella's turn to sigh.

'The authorities can do anything they please; you must at least have learned that by now, Lottie? This could stop the US of A investing in our film business. And that is serious. Any hint of someone being left-wing and film people all become hysterical.'

That brought my fantasy to an abrupt halt. Not that I would have had an affair with a star while I was still in tandem with Harry, absolutely not. But you know how it goes. Your mind can wander off the straight and narrow sometimes, and I had once seen one of this particular star's pictures three times. He was that kind of draw.

'I don't suppose he is really a communist, probably just said something like he thinks poor people should have food on the table, which scared the liver and lights out of the studios.'

'Quite. But that does not bring us any nearer to helping Zuzu.'

Arabella gave me her best deep look to remind me that I was now tasked with confronting my father about it, which would not be easy.

'Can't help much,' he said with some finality. 'She forgot the rule, you see, Lottie – mustn't frat with the enemy – serious stuff. She'll probably be asked to leave the service. You know, get the sack.'

I didn't like my father mentioning a sack, because Harry was always sure that if you were on the wrong side of the authorities they put you in one – with some added ballast, of course – and by-mistake-on-purpose dropped you into the swirling water of the Thames.

'However, I'll do what I can.'

My father looked dubious and turned away before turning back.

'Of course, you could do something to help this friend of yours,' he said suddenly. 'That would probably be better. Get on the right side of her – find out more about this chap, always the best way – get in close, watch his habits, make notes, etc. What he likes, who he talks to, where he dines out.'

'Oh, I don't think I would be very good at that,' I said, too quickly.

'In that case, nothing to be done. Your friend may well end up in dickie's meadow.'

All my childhood I had never been able to find out where dickie's meadow was, but I always knew from the way my father referred to it that it was somewhere nice people would not want to be.

'I'll do what I can, then,' I said, knowing that it was the last thing I wanted.

I went up to my room and lay on my bed and thought of how awful it was going to be. I would be spying on a friend, and not just a friend – on Zuzu, but if it was the only way to get her off some draconian punishment that would end up with her being force-fed like suffragettes, so be it. Of course Arabella had to be in on it. Very little in my life worked if I didn't let Arabella in on my plans. It was not that she was all-wise and all-seeing, it was because she had the one thing that Harry and I lacked – common sense.

'As the great man said, there is too little of it about for it to be common,' Harry always intoned.

Arabella had advised against Harry being part of any plan as far as Zuzu went, and of course she was right, but it was very difficult to hatch a plan without him getting suspicious. He had this way of knowing things you hadn't told him, so much so that I sometimes felt it was dangerous even to think in front of him. I suppose this all came about from our working together, but whatever the reason it was very constraining.

Not that I told Arabella this. I just agreed not to tell Harry anything in case he was disgusted that I was willing to spy on a friend. He hadn't been too happy about our part in infiltrating a certain well-known actor's house. It had been against his principles and he had only carried it off because he was an actor, and not a bloated capitalist. Harry did not like bloated capitalists, feeling that they did not add to the beauty of things. Myself, I was all for them as long as they backed films and plays.

As it happened I was right, and Harry being Harry he was on to it immediately.

'It's something to do with Zuzu?'

'A bit.'

'How big a bit?'

'A sizeable bit – more a chunk really. Perhaps you could come too?'

'I have been booked for a radio play, big names involved. Poets and playwrights that you usually only see on volumes of classic literary output in university libraries.'

I kissed Harry because I was impressed by his coping with ancient poets, but he wasn't paying much attention so I carried on with my plan to meet Zuzu at the star's penthouse in Mayfair. I can tell you, I was in dread, so it was all I could do to leave.

The reason I was in dread was that I feared that Zuzu, by dint of her involvement, would have become somehow less. Perhaps it was for this reason that I took Arabella with me and because she knew so much more about everything, and even if she didn't she always looked as if she did. The penthouse was knee-deep in white carpet as we discovered when the French maid opened the door to us.

We snowshoed our way through to the drawing room where we could hear the deep tones of the star and the lighter ones of Zuzu in what was obviously an important discussion.

The atmosphere in the room was one to which I would eventually become used, but on this occasion it struck me as being almost eerie. It was as if life outside the windows was not taking place: there were no taxis drawing up in rhythmic succession, there were no meals being ordered in the famous restaurant downstairs, there was in short nothing going on except the life of the star, and his presence was filling the whole room. Or he certainly thought it was. And here's a thing: I knew from Arabella's best and most Gandhi-like expression as soon as she saw Zuzu that she had indeed changed.

She was even more Zuzu than before.

'Sir', as Zuzu called him, had an authority all of his own making, a huge glass of something alcoholically lethal in one hand, an untipped cigarette burning away in the other. When he greeted us his voice was immensely impressive, deep cello notes bouncing across the room so that even 'hello' sounded positively Shakespearean.

Yet he was as nothing compared to Zuzu. It was immediately obvious that her aura far outshone his.

'Sir must eat early on account of studio hours,' she explained, pursing her lips, which was one of her specialities. 'You'll join us, of course.'

Arabella and I declined. My reason for declining was that when faced with an ego as large as that of Sir, I would not be able to swallow a morsel, and I like swallowing morsels. Not even lobster mayonnaise would tempt me to stay, and yet we both knew we had to stay for a little to collar Zuzu.

Arabella and I perched on the squashy sofas, staring at him pacing about the room smoking and drinking and opining while Zuzu bossed her eyes at us.

He stopped suddenly.

'Why are you ladies laughing? Are you laughing? Is there something amusing happening?'

'Only because Sir is being so amusing,' Zuzu put in quickly, to cover for us.

He thought for a minute.

'Yes, you're right, I am amusing,' he agreed.

An intense-looking woman came into the room bearing with her a couple of scripts. Zuzu clapped her hands. 'Time for Sir to do his homework.'

'Oh, God, must I? Some of the lines are so dead, I swear not even Olivier could revive them.'

Sir took a deep draught of his drink at the same time as pulling on his cigarette, a feat that always leaves me feeling a vague admiration.

Zuzu indicated that we could leave Sir's presence now, and we followed her into the lift and downstairs to the bar, which suddenly seemed like an oasis of normality.

'So – who sent you?'

Arabella looked calm at this, eyes unmoving, while I cleared my throat and looked mortified.

'The usuals.'

'I am on leave, all above board as far as the powers that be are concerned.'

'Absolutely,' I said, sounding creepy.

'So where's the smoke drifting from? Why are the drums beating?'

Zuzu ordered champagne cocktails and smiled, and I knew at once that all was not as it seemed. It was *that* smile. The one she turned on Monty that always had him spinning round and dusting the very heavens for her.

Arabella responded after only a sip of her cocktail. 'A grub is on to you.'

I frowned. They were talking serious Section talk now, which was out of my league.

Zuzu stopped smiling and lit a cigarette in her usual elegant way. 'A lowly grub or a great fat grub?'

'A big fat one. Writes for a distinguished newspaper and wants to drag the security service through the mud, denigrate the work, generally cause mirth and derision at our expense. You know the type: mixes with people whom he despises, ears flapping, eyes that can see around doors while he stays in the room. Very successful at it, so he gets asked everywhere.'

Long before Arabella mentioned his name she had rather lost me, except for one thing – this so-called grub was obviously pretty horrid.

Zuzu drew on her cigarette, sipped her champagne cocktail, and looked from one to the other of us, her eyes sparkling.

'What's his angle?'

'Mata Hari, of course,' Arabella said briefly.

At that Zuzu gave her best gurgling laugh. Once again I thought of Monty and how he would raise his wig in delight when he heard that sound, and murmur, 'Mademoiselle, oh, mademoiselle, oh, the delight of you.'

'Oh, but this is such fun,' Zuzu said. 'We can have such fun with this.'

Arabella and I looked at each other in some astonishment. Even I knew that people did not have fun with important grubs. Grub Strasse, as Melville called Fleet Street, always, but always, had the last word. It was just a fact.

'Never fight the newspapers,' was my father's terse comment if the matter was ever raised at Dingley Dell.

'So here's how,' Zuzu said, and she took a hotel napkin and drew an arrow on it. 'One of you take him for a drink, and beg him, and I mean *beg* him, not to break the story that I am having a huge affair with Sir. You will exaggerate my role in the War Office; mention in passing that my father was a celebrated wartime agent, and so on. Meanwhile I will do what I do best – and make mischief.'

'It's why you were placed on Planet Earth,' Arabella agreed.

Zuzu then said, 'You will take him for a drink,' looking at both of us, but I suddenly realised that she meant me.

'I can't take grubs for drinks, Zuzu,' I said, feeling quite faint just at the thought.

'Of course you can—'

'No,' Arabella put in swiftly. 'She can't. She'll make a hash of it.'

I was never more grateful that Arabella knew just what a twerp I was. Zuzu considered this, and then nodded slowly.

'Yes, you're right, Arabella, and anyway you're more beautiful.'

The gratitude that I felt for my two friends' appreciation of my limitations knew no bounds.

'Will you be all right?' I asked Arabella later as we waited for the bus.

'Of course I will, my mother knows him. He came to one of her evenings not long ago. Monty didn't take to him, so he put the chap's mink-lined Mackintosh in the kitchen scraps bin.'

'Not really?'

'Yes, really – he sent it on later, but only after he had told the Grub that someone else must have gone off with it, which made him wait in an agony of uncertainty. He's good like that, Monty.'

I felt more than relieved, I felt reprieved.

'So the plan is simple, yes?' I asked, trying not to sound anxious.

'Yes, it is simple,' Arabella agreed. 'Mother is away in Italy – she is looking for new recipes for Monty who hates to travel. He is in charge at the flat.'

'Does he know about Zuzu being back?'

'I hope not,' Arabella said, curtly, as she hopped on the bus and I followed and we sat on the back seat for three. 'We can't have Monty knowing, at least not yet – he will start to polish Rollo even more than he does already.'

*

I felt I ought to find out more about our man, so I caught up with my father just after he had poured himself a stiffy.

'What sort of person is this terribly important grub?'

'He's a bit of a lounge lizard so best to have some-one with you when he's about,' said my father, lighting a cigarette and wandering off into the garden.

'Apparently he might pounce,' I told Arabella. 'So how about if I come in halfway through, or near the end?'

'But we don't know when the end will be, Lottie,' she said in the kind voice she always used to me, before adding, 'oh, very well, but only at the end of the first hour. I'll see him at the flat.'

I couldn't leave it at that, because leaving things to take their course was not my way, unfortunately, so I got Monty to let me in the service entrance and then hung about the kitchen, getting under his feet and eating his carefully prepared cocktail snacks while imagining how Arabella was getting on.

'Why she would want that excuse for a man to come visiting I wouldn't know,' Monty said, snorting lightly, and sighing.

I looked at the string of onions hung over the stove and I too sighed because staring at onions is the only thing to do when you know the answer to something.

Later I looked at the clock and saw that the first hour must be up. 'Ready for the off, are you, Miss Lottie?' Monty asked, as I put on some lipstick and he held the mirror. 'You don't want to do too much primping,' he went on in a disapproving tone. 'The creature in there might get the wrong idea. Now off you go, and don't say too much.'

I thought I was quite on top of everything until Monty showed me into the drawing room, when I instantly realised that I was completely unprepared for the scene in front of me.

The Grub, seated on one of Arabella's mother's squishy sofas, was coddled up in his fur-lined Mackintosh, and not unnaturally sweating for the fire was lit and the room very warm. I realised instantly that the reason he was keeping his grub garb on was because he was in mortal fear it would disappear again. I almost felt sorry for him, for not only was he a rather sodden grub, but it seemed to me that he emanated a strangely inhuman smell, which must be a result of the mink-lined Mac's stint in Monty's kitchen bin.

'We are finished here,' he told me, 'so don't mind me – go ahead and talk girlie talk.'

I looked across at Arabella and knew at once that she was feeling very un-Gandhi-like. This was most particularly apparent because her delicate nostrils were flaring. She did not like people referring to her as a 'girlie'. It did not go down well.

She glanced at the clock, and I knew that she must be calculating what was happening elsewhere with Zuzu. This became more than obvious when she embarked on a long conversation about fashion models she knew who were very much in the news at that moment, the papers all saying they were the Gaiety Girls of their generation because so many of them had married into the aristocracy.

At the same time as the conversation turned to matters that would normally have bored Arabella senseless, she rang for Monty and ordered more cocktails, which were duly delivered and drunk far too quickly by the Grub whose condition had become quite feverish due to his devotion to his horrible Mackintosh.

At last he staggered to his feet, but not before Monty had plied him with more of the same.

'Must go and file—' he said, happily. 'Thank you for your story, most illuminating.'

Once again I almost felt sorry for him. Even though I had no idea how he was going to be turned over by that will o' the wisp, the Tinkerbell of the Secret Service known as Zuzu – I just knew he would not stand a chance.

Arabella was far too well trained to let me know what the outcome of her interview might be, and so I had to be content to travel home by bus wondering what was going to happen next.

I was due to meet Harry at our coffee bar. He was there ahead of me, but not sitting in front of a coffee; he was sitting in front of something much stronger. I was already quite nicely thank you because of Monty's cocktails so I contented myself with a coffee, and waited to hear about Harry's experiences on BBC radio with the kind of poets and writers whose work is normally only found between leatherbound volumes in discreet libraries.

'Well?' I said.

'Well, as in well, well, well – here's a fine kettle of fish.'

At work, when writing together, we had a pact never to use 'well' in dialogue, so it seemed almost shocking now that we were both using it in real life.

'How did it go with all the illustrious poets and playwrights at the BBC?'

Harry gave me a deep look.

'They were all wonderful – marvellous – funny – brilliant—'

I knew the 'and' word would be good here, so I took a punt and used it. 'And?'

'Drunk as skunks.'

I was intrigued.

'How so?'

'How do you think, Lottie? From drinking alcohol, and as soon as they arrived. And their producer – a lovely man – was the same. Footless, opening the gin bottle at half-past ten. I thought: *We're never going to get through the work if this is how it is.* But do you know?' He sighed. 'We did, and what is more, and what is so – so – amazing, they were better than anything or anyone I have ever worked with.'

I let out a sigh of satisfaction before ordering another coffee because Monty's cocktails were beginning to have a latent hammering effect.

'I suppose it is only to be expected that the artistic temperament requires stimulus, like Coleridge writing "The Ancient Mariner" on drugs, that sort of thing?'

Harry shook his head.

'You're not getting it, Lottie. The point is, if they can be so brilliant while plastered, is this the way forward for the rest of us? I mean could alcohol be the answer to everything?'

I felt it important to consider this as Harry took a gulp of his drink. 'I think you have to be brilliant to get drunk and still be brilliant,' I offered, at my most philosophical. 'But if you and I got drunk, because we're not brilliant we would simply get drunk.'

'How dreary, Lottie.'

I frowned. Of course Harry was right, it was a dreary thought, but on the other hand, who was to say that all these immortals of our times were happy?

'Of course they're happy. If you're brilliant you are always happy,' Harry stated, firmly.

'That's my point,' I said, quickly. 'We have to strive to be brilliant, and stay sober, to be happy.'

'It's all so ordinary.'

Harry was not often miserable, at least not to the naked eye, but I could see he was miserable now. That all these brilliant, funny people had made his own life seem dull and ordinary. They had lowered the temperature for him. They had certainly lowered mine, and then I remembered how, when Zuzu had come into my life and then was gone again, I had felt the same way. Harry needed something to raise him up again after keeping company with the Gods of Literature and Poetry, after being with the immortals, but what that might be I could not say. I realised I was too close to him to help him. Anyway I had too many hammers applying themselves to my head.

Harry left me at Dingley Dell and wended his way back to flat-sharing with Dermot and all, and I slid into the house in my usual way, which was through the dining-room window so as not to be noticed, only what with one thing and another – and certainly Monty's cocktails had not helped – I found myself marooned behind the dining-room curtains just as one of my mother's dinner parties was ending.

Talk about stuck behind the arras.

The talk went on for a while, broken up eventually by the usual chorus of: 'Is that really the time?'

Once they had all retired upstairs, I slipped out of the dining room and into the kitchen where I knew my mother always left the *Evening Standard* for Mrs Graham to read with her first coffee in the morning.

I opened the paper. There it was, the full story. It seemed that the very famous star had been found by his long-lost sister, namely Zuzu, after many years of searching. They had both been sent to America as part of the children's wartime exodus. Once there they had been parted, and following the death of their parents during the war, sister and brother had lost touch. Zuzu had found her long-lost brother while working for the War Office, after which she had brought him to England to re-establish his career by making a patriotic war film in which he played a heroic pilot.

I stared round the kitchen with happy satisfaction. The saucepans had never looked more cheerful, nor the rows of cream-coloured tins with words like 'Sago' written on them more homely and comforting. Everything now became beautifully clear to me. Zuzu and Arabella had trapped the Grub by spinning him the wrong story while making sure the true story came out before his.

It all seemed magnificently simple, and of course really rather brilliant, although I myself felt a little shabby to think that I had believed Zuzu could become entangled with a movie star. She was above movie stars, she was Zuzu, Mademoiselle, the meteor from Section XXX.

Unfortunately my euphoria did nothing for Harry, who not so secretly resented Zuzu, because like the illustrious immortals he had met at the BBC she lit up lives with a special aura he suspected we might not have.

I have to say, I confided Harry's vaguely disquieting discontent to Zuzu next time we met, which was out to a celebration dinner in the countryside, chauffeured there by Monty in Rollo who was in shining form, as was Monty, stars in his eyes now that Mademoiselle was in our midst once again, for however little time.

As I chatted to Zuzu I realised Arabella was looking on, her expression serious. We both knew that Harry needed something big to get him out of what was threatening to become a pit of despair.

'A touch of adventure in the Wild Wood is what young Harry needs,' Arabella murmured at one point. 'Something frightening to make him rein back and realise how lucky he is.'

Zuzu took the point; I knew this because her eyes were changing colour, always a potent moment.

I think it was the mention of an adventure in the Wild Wood that did it. We all knew that the Wild Wood, full of unknown danger, existed for everyone in some form or another, but how to place Harry in his, to take him out of his melancholy, was not immediately apparent, at least not to me.

Zuzu finally gave her best 'got just the thing' smile, and we left it at that. The rest of the evening passed very pleasantly indeed, and I returned to Dingley Dell confident that something would occur that would help Harry. The only trouble being that I had, in my innocence, assumed I would be left out of Harry's projected cure. I had no need or desire to have my spirits lifted. I was more than happy already. Between them Zuzu and Arabella had defeated the Grub and put paid to the swirling rumours. The sun was shining and Mrs Graham had just finished making some crunchy ice cream.

It was only when the telephone on my desk at MI5 rang and it was Harry that I remembered the mischief in Zuzu's smile, and how her eyes had changed colour as she'd thought of the best way to help him out of his depressed state. My heart sank.

Harry was not going into the Wild Wood alone — I was going too.

INTO THE WILD WOOD

I once saw a writer coming out of a very famous film
producer's office. His expensive suit was creased in a
very unromantic way, and he was carrying the kind of
briefcase that I later realised successful writers tend
to carry – leather and vaguely authoritative – which
when opened usually reveals nothing more exciting
than a much-thumbed script and a spare pair of socks.
I was only at the producer's smart office to drop off a
parcel from my father. The film was being made very
close to the Iron Curtain, which as far as my father was
concerned was very useful indeed. I guessed the parcel
was probably going to be left in a dead letter box, so I
signed the delivery book, putting the parcel's contents
down as 'lace doilies', and silently wished whatever it
was inside a happy landing, and that was that.

My errand was easy enough, but the sight of that
sighing grey-faced film writer haunted me. Was this
what happened when you wrote for films? I quickly
came to the conclusion that the film writer must be

a bit of a sad sack, and decidedly lacking in what Mrs Graham always called 'gumption'. Why else would he look as though he was going home to have tea with the KGB?

All this happened long before I discovered what Zuzu had planned for Harry, and therefore, as night followed day, for me.

It was, on the face of it, a great act of kindness on Zuzu's behalf and one to which Monty referred a great deal. More than a great deal actually. As far as he was concerned Mademoiselle had done Harry and me a great, great favour, but then Monty was not a budding writer. All he knew was that Zuzu, through her many contacts in the film world, had secured for us, two unknown scribblers, an interview with a highly regarded film director. Well, not so much highly regarded, as very, very famous, which I subsequently discovered in the film world really means the same thing.

Harry too could hardly believe it. In fact, his state of disbelief was such that he could not bring himself to tell Dermot or anyone else at the flat, or indeed anyone at all, which I decided was just as well. What was in the offing had to be a state secret or Dermot and everyone would start to pitch in and point out why Harry and I should not go up for the job.

Then Monty told us we would never get a job with the famous Bennett Hunter if we looked too poor. It seemed in order to get the job we had to make a great impression of being much employed and above all opulent.

I wasn't too sure about this, but when I told Harry he agreed with Monty that no one ever wanted to have anything to do with someone who was poor and needy. It was just the way of the world. People only wanted to help people who didn't need it. Between them they settled on Monty wearing a smart suit and chauffeur's cap, polishing up Rollo and driving us round to the great man's house, a private mansion in leafy West London.

Rollo had never looked so smart, Monty too, so much so that in contrast Harry and I, seated in the back, looked more than a bit on the shabby side, but I comforted myself with the thought that writers should always look only nearly new, rather than fresh out of Harrods, because it meant that they were too busy with deep thoughts to care much for appearances. That was my fond belief and I stuck to it, or rather clung to it, as Monty carefully parked Rollo, and the front door of the mansion was opened to us by an immaculately uniformed maid.

Unfortunately the maid was not alone. Directly behind her stood the terribly famous director – Bennett Hunter. I knew he was the director even though he wasn't sitting in a chair with *Direct*or written on the back of it, because he was holding a megaphone, which he now used, most effectively, to speak to the maid who went off looking very cross and French which so often amounts to the same thing.

Bennett Hunter lowered his megaphone.

'I have to use this on her because she doesn't understand English.' He nodded at us. 'I need no introduction, obviously,' he went on. 'One of the few perks about being so famous is that you need no introduction.'

Harry introduced us.

'We will retire to the drawing room now, my dears.'

The sunken drawing room was swathed in evening light, which highlighted the pale blue silk-lined walls, which in turn were hung with gilt-framed paintings.

'Please be seated, my dears,' Mr Hunter said, indicating that we could sit opposite him, after which he placed the megaphone to his lips, shouting, 'Bring in the drinks, Hortense.'

Another maid, also crisply dressed, ventured down some steps. On a mahogany coffee tray she placed an exquisitely laid silver salver set with cocktail glasses and bottles boasting foreign labels, a cut-crystal ice bowl and gold tongs.

'You two are the tenth writers or writing partnership I have seen in the last twenty-four hours,' he announced. 'There does not seem to be a great deal of film work about in England these days.'

We stared at him feeling duly humbled.

'So how do you feel about working for me?'

I left that one to Harry.

'Intrigued,' he said, after a short pause during which I knew he was rejecting anything that might sound too craven or – worse – grateful.

'I too am intrigued.' Bennett Hunter nodded. 'Now remind me of your names?'

'Of course, Mr Hunter, it's very easy to get us muddled – I am Harry, shorter hair, deeper voice. This person here with long hair and lipstick is Lottie.'

It was then something extraordinary happened. Bennett Hunter laughed, and he did not just laugh – he cracked up.

'Oh, dear, oh, dear, I fear I am easily pleased at this juncture of a very long day. Out of an endless line of ******* writers, you are the first ******* writers to come through my front door and make me laugh,' he said, wiping his eyes with a handkerchief that had BH embroidered above what looked like a hand. 'My dears, sit down, sit down!'

'We are sitting down.'

'In that case, stay down.'

More laughter during which I tried not to gaze around the opulent room.

Roland Andrews' house had been swanky in a theatrical way but this was Hollywood empirical.

Happily, on the way there we had both agreed that we would never get the job. This made us collectively carefree.

'You have never written a movie, I daresay, my dears?'

We agreed we had not.

'Why do you think that is?'

'Two reasons,' Harry said smoothly, and at once, which gave the impression that we had been asked this many times. 'First we are not American, and secondly we want to see our work on-screen as it was written, and there is small chance of that in the film world.'

'Not a small chance – no chance whatsoever. My dear Lottie, my dear Harry, I will tell you now, you will never see your work reproduced as you have written it on a screen.'

This seemed to delight Harry, who immediately started to get up off the squishy sofa.

He held out his hand to Bennett Hunter.

'Thank you very much for seeing us, Mr Hunter. And we both wish you the best of luck for the future.'

I struggled up off the sofa and held out my hand too, but he took neither, only shaking his head impatiently.

'Sit down, my dears ... Lottie, Harry, sit down. There is no need to rush out. We have only just begun our parley, only just begun.'

I glanced at Harry. He sat down, so I too sat down, at the same time experiencing an inexplicable feeling of disappointment. I thought it would have been such a brilliant move to leave before being turned down anyway.

'You two are very volatile, both of you, very volatile. I haven't yet explained what it is I want you to write. And if you write it as I wish, who knows? You may even see your work on-screen, its integrity intact. The impossible does sometimes happen as we know from watching Hollywood films!'

'We don't want to keep you, Mr Hunter.'

'Good, good, so many people do,' he said, and appearing to think we had caved in he went to pick up his megaphone, but then changed his mind.

'Please pour the drinks, Mr Harry Writer,' he said to Harry.

Now one of Harry's many strengths was that he was brilliant at pouring drinks on account of having to work in bars when he was short of money.

'What would you like, Mr Hunter?'

Bennett Hunter gave him a long look.

'What do you think I would like, my dear Harry?'

Harry stared at him, frowning.

'You're like Billy Wilder,' he finally announced. 'You enjoy a mean Martini.'

Bennett Hunter gave a satisfied smile.

'My dear friend Billy drank ten Martinis at the Oscars last year. It was the record, but he still didn't get best director – just a headache. He has over fifty pairs of tennis shoes. I have sixty-five. I remind him of that every time we meet.'

Harry's Martinis were so mean that after only a few sips I began to see Mr Hunter's face not just in Technicolor but in triple vision.

'Now what do my dear Harry and my dear Lottie know about movies and the movie business?'

Once again I let Harry speak, mainly because what I knew about films could be written on the back of a postage stamp.

'First of all,' he said, eventually, 'you need to set your film somewhere movie stars want to go – say, the South of France, or – or Venice.'

Bennett Hunter beamed. Actually he did better than that: he radiated contentment at Harry, and I could see Harry caught in the beam.

'My dear Harry, is your father in the business?'

He thought for a minute. Even I found myself intrigued as to what his answer might be. Harry's father worked in the City for an investment company, played golf at the weekend and went to church on Sunday, so from the little I knew of him, I could not imagine him having anything to do with movies.

'My father *invests*,' Harry said, giving an almost sinister emphasis to the word.

'I like gentlemen who invest. Does he invest a great deal?'

'Oh, yes,' Harry said blithely. 'He puts money in all sorts of things, beer, food, shipping, you know how it is in the City.'

I later found out this was quite true but at that moment I was sure that Harry was busking it.

'Movies even?'

Harry smiled.

'Oh, I expect so,' he said, and his smile was huge.

'I like this father of yours, my dear Harry,' Mr Hunter told us. 'I like him very much. So it was probably from this shrewd man that you learned the first truth about movie stars: they like to holiday when they work, so forget the studios, take them on location to glamorous places. Never mind the script, just find the right hotel!'

I have led a very sheltered life, so I felt shocked at the idea that actors would choose films for their locations rather than their precious artistic content.

'My dear Lottie is looking astonished at our news, Mr Harry Writer. No, she is looking *bouleversé,* as they say in La France, or did when I was last there filming with dear Gina. What a gal! She did my movie because it was set in gay Paree. So that exactly illustrates our point.'

Harry smiled.

'If it was so appealing to Gina Lalalalala – why not go again with Paris once more for your new movie, Mr Hunter?'

A loud sound broke out in the room. I stared, trying to focus through the alco-vision of the mean Martini. The sound was Bennett Hunter clapping.

'Now I know you are part of the movie family, Mr Harry Writer, because only a member calls the beautiful Gina that. And, yes, you are right. We shall go again with our new movie to gay Paree. That suits me so well, because it means I can get home to do my laundry of an evening, should I need to.'

For a second I thought Harry's Martini had gone to my ears, but no, it seemed Mr Hunter's laundry was sacred to him.

'I can trust no one else with my garments,' he continued. Harry nodded happily at this as if he felt the same.

'Quite right, quite right, Mr Hunter. There is always a feeling of helplessness when you hand your best shirt over to a maid who is probably about to leave your service.'

Bennett Hunter stared at Harry as if he was the US cavalry come over the hill at just the right moment. This time he did not smile, he did not laugh – he purred.

I looked from one to the other and my heart sank once again. It was obvious that Bennett Hunter had fallen in love with Harry. He finished his mean Martini and rose to his feet. Harry rose to his. I rose only to one foot and then the other, very carefully, to cover any overt swaying that might follow.

'I will show you to the door,' Bennett Hunter announced.

It was only very much later that I realised that this was a great Hollywood-style compliment. '*I will show you to the lift*' means that, barring accidents, you are more or less signed.

Monty, standing beside Rollo, was waiting for us in the drive wearing his best. He raised his cap at Bennett Hunter who smiled.

'I like writers with style,' he murmured.

We had hardly climbed into Rollo before I started to worry about what would happen if we got the job. We had no experience of writing for what you could call proper films. You could hardly call our work on *Sexy Aliens* the right experience for dealing with someone like Bennett Hunter. As I sat voicing my jitters, Harry put on his not-listening-to-a-word face and stared contentedly out of the window.

'He'll sign us,' he announced finally. 'And you know what swung it for us? The bit about the laundry. I knew from some old interview that he does his own washing and always has. He has a thing about germs. That is why he uses the megaphone, so as not to get too near the person he wants to talk to. Notice he did not shake hands? If he has to go anywhere he wears gloves, like the Queen.'

'Not those long evening gloves?'

'You wait and see if we don't get the job.'

*

The next day, back at my proper job in my Section at MI5, I confided my fears to Arabella, who threw me a bored look, which I caught.

'My dear Lottie—' she began.

'Oh, don't say that, Arabella,' I moaned. 'Please don't, you sound just like Bennett Hunter.'

Arabella smiled.

'He has a terrible reputation for bullying writers, and actors too,' she said contentedly. 'Many stars have walked off the set on account of his megaphone manners.'

'I know,' I said. 'He even uses it when speaking to the maid.'

Arabella looked ever-more content.

'Lottie,' she said with a sigh, 'Zuzu in her infinite wisdom has swung you an interview with a very famous director and all you are doing is moaning. You should be ashamed of yourself. Harry has stopped feeling miserable, I daresay, you might be going to write a movie in Paris for famous, famous stars – and yet here you are, looking as if you are about to receive a prison sentence.'

I was duly humbled, and when I felt like a worm without earth I always went in to see Commander Steerforth because in my eyes he was a saint who had fought the war and come out of it with a love for everything proper, because after all, as he always said – we did win it.

'Victoria sponge?' I asked him brightly.

'Not just before lunch, thank you, Lottie,' he said in a kind voice, handing me back a memo I had taken down wrong. 'How's the scribbling going?'

It had become a running joke between us to refer to my scribbling with Harry as 'night work' and myself as a night worker, which for some reason we both continued to find funny; because due to not trapping any spies lately, little jokes helped relieve the lack of tension. Still, we all hoped something exciting would happen to occupy us pretty soon, although my father seemed to think that communism was losing. And of course commercials selling cheerful products, apparently it had all had the effect of making people less cross.

'The night job,' I finally answered, 'is in the pending tray.'

We laughed and I scurried back to my desk only to find that Arabella had answered my phone and it was Harry calling.

'The news is that that even now Dewi is negotiating with the famous cheese, apparently.'

I sank down into my chair, clutching my files and staring at Arabella. 'Let's go and celebrate at Fenwick's,' she suggested.

I nodded dumbly while silently praying that Dewi would make a hash of the negotiations. Agents negotiating contracts with very important people are usually very important themselves. I was sure that Dewi, even if he put out his cigarettes, or his cigars, and concentrated hard, would not be up to Mr Bennett Hunter, who was more used to dealing with Hollywood agents. So after a long day re-typing memos I had done wrong, and plying the Commander with Victoria sponge, I caught the bus home in the kind of mood I imagined comes upon a person who has had a prison sentence quashed. Dewi would make a hash of it. I was as sure of that as I was that Mrs Graham would be cooking beef at the weekend and Melville playing the piano and Hal booming at my mother about theatre.

I was so confident that I began a new script about an impoverished writer who gets left a Rolls-Royce like Rollo by an old American lady he had been driving round England prior to her going back to the States, where she lived with a crowd of ungrateful relatives.

It always made me feel very happy to be making a start on a new script. The blank piece of paper seemed to beckon me on to new adventures, taking my mind off everything else.

I had hardly typed *MERRILY IT ROLLS ALONG by Lottie Burrell*, when someone knocked at the door and it was my mother, wearing her best martyred look.

'Er – Harry is on the telephone,' she said in a tone that indicated his call to our house was interfering with government matters of a serious nature.

I rushed downstairs, hoping against hope that Dewi would not have made a deal with Mr Hunter.

'Lottie,' Harry said, and his voice had a quiet authority. 'The deal was done, in five minutes flat. Mr Bennett Hunter told Dewi that he knew we were the right people for him and we would be admirably suited. He is sending a contract tomorrow and the money will be in the bank before you can say Gina Lalalala.'

'I don't think I have any more leave left, at least not enough,' I said, thinking quickly that maybe if I hadn't got any left, Harry would have to cope on his own.

'You won't need any, that is what is so great. He is in the middle of something else, editing it and so on – so he doesn't want us round until after six.'

'After six?' I said. 'But what about his washing – he said that's how he spends his evenings, doing his washing.'

Harry laughed.

'I don't think that's in the contract – yet. See you for coffee, Lottie-bags.'

My mother had followed me downstairs. She stared at the telephone receiver as I replaced it.

'Bad news about the film?' she asked, hopefully.

'Yes,' I said. 'I'm afraid we have been contracted.'

My mother stared at me for a few seconds.

'Well, if you will do these things, Lottie,' she said finally, 'you will find that's what happens. Anyway, your father will be pleased. He likes to know about these people. Keeps a tab on them.'

I frowned at her. Was there nothing MI5 wasn't interested in?

'This is the worst bit,' Harry stated as I slid onto the bench seat opposite him and ordered a coffee. 'You realise we now have to write the film, and we have to set it in Paris, and neither of us knows a thing about Paris.'

I nodded, thinking of the script I had started, and wishing that I was going to write that rather than something for Mr Hunter. It wasn't something I could tell Harry about. I led a secret life on my typewriter, the results of which I kept undercover in a coded folder, probably because Harry did not always agree with what old Hollywood would call my *weenies* – so I felt it was better to keep them in the Top Secret File.

'Doesn't matter that we don't know Paris, there are books on it, aren't there? You don't need to know about a place to write about it. My father had a friend who wrote a bestseller called *On Foot Through the Himalayas* and he'd never left Chipping Camden.'

Harry looked shocked.

'Your family know some very strange people, Lottie.'

I stared out of the window at some very odd-looking passers-by. It was true. My family did know a great many odd people. They probably knew some of the people who had just gone by the window. I thought about the script I was writing at home. It was not set in Paris. Actually it was not set anywhere at the moment. The hero, if he could be called such, had only just found the advertisement in an old evening newspaper left on the seat beside him on the number nine bus.

'Lottie, you are meant to be listening to me.'

'I am listening to you, Harry.'

'We are meant to be talking about working for this great director everyone knows is very famous, except perhaps for you.'

I saw my moment. Harry, I realised, knew me well enough to see that my heart was not in writing for Mr Bennett Hunter, however famous.

'If we are going to do this – this picture for Mr Hunter – we must have an incentive in our minds, something that we really, really want.'

'How do you mean? Like getting Dermot to wash up?'

'Something like – say – a motor car.'

'A *motor car* forsooth, if not fifthsooth?' Harry mocked.

I ignored him. I like old-fashioned words like wireless and motor car and luncheon. They make me think of boating on the Thames, and men opening doors for you and standing up when you left the table.

'Actually, Harry,' I said, clearing my throat so he knew I meant what I was about to say.

'Actually – Lottie?'

'I would like a motor car, and I will not write a word if you do not agree to putting whatever few shillings Dewi has got us towards one.'

'Very well, I will put mine towards a car – you can put yours towards a motor car.'

'Remember those words, Harry, you will need to, believe me.'

Harry smiled. He was too full of the moment to pick me up on my implied threat, but then he had not witnessed the film writer coming out of the producer's office that day. He did not know what was in store for us, whereas I was quite sure I did.

There the evening ended – well, more or less, except for Harry insisting on going back to his flat and opening a bottle of Italian wine – the kind that people always use afterwards to put candles in – and singing along to his guitar. It was fine until Dermot came in and Harry forgot himself so far as to tell him that we had just collared a film to write, which of course sent Dermot to bed in a paroxysm of fury, charging us with being tainted with capitalist values from which he predicted we would never recover.

The following evening, spruced up for our first appointment with the great man, we agreed not to ask

Monty to drive us to his mansion but to walk round while discussing the story we might write.

As before the maid opened the front door, and as before Mr Bennett Hunter was lurking about the hall, this time not with his megaphone, but a packet of washing powder tucked under his arm.

'I've just done the first load, always measure the soap myself,' he said, beaming, and thrust the packet at the maid who continued to look French and cross. '*Voulez-vous* please get behind the drinks trolley *toute suite, ma bonne* Hortense?'

I glanced at Harry. Drinking while writing was not something we did. It was just not ethical. However, I immediately saw an opening. We could refuse to drink and write, then take our leave at once. I imagined us being very dignified. Telling all our friends how committed we had been. Dermot might even admire us for our stand. It could be good.

'Mr Hunter – we never drink until after we have written. It is a rule.'

'Of course you don't, Mr Harry Writer,' Bennett Hunter agreed. 'But tonight you are not writing, you are entertaining me. We are celebrating our contract together. Before I leave you for a few moments to make sure all is well in the laundry room, Mr Harry Writer, will you do the honours by making us Billy Wilder's favourite drink, eh? While he does so, my dear Lottie will tell me a few of her weenies for this film we will shoot in Paris *sur* Seine. No doubt there will be *bateaux* mooches involved and of course the Ritz Hotel.'

Even I knew that the Ritz in Paris housed a bar which all the American and many English writers and journalists liked to drink each other under — while telling themselves they were doing valuable research.

I even remembered that Hal knew some of them.

'A bunch of old soaks who think they're amusing because their editors print "from our witty Paris correspondent" at the top of their weekly columns,' he'd boomed. 'And one of them threatened my sister with writing a lousy review of her book unless she went upstairs with him. She left before the melon, bless her.'

'Well, of course we will involve the Ritz Hotel, Mr Hunter,' I agreed, taking my Martini from Harry. 'But first we have to decide will our hero have the camera on his shoulder, or will it be coming towards him? Technically that is what we have to establish first, you will agree?'

As I finished speaking there was the sound of something being dropped.

It was Harry's jaw.

'My dear Lottie, I see and hear you speak *Cahiers du Cinéma*,' Mr Hunter purred.

I could do nothing of the sort. But since I was quite small I had made a point of reading Mrs Graham's *Movie Weekly*. Recently there had been an interview with a famous French director in which he said that sort of thing.

'Of course, the French influence is very much *à la mode* at the moment,' Harry put in, quickly.

'How long can it last, Mr Hunter?' I asked, looking grave but innocent, a look I was intent on perfecting. 'How long will audiences want to sit through subtitles, or follow balloons through the streets of Paris? How long?'

Mr Hunter was getting excited, but just as he was about to opine the pinger on his watch went off and it was obviously a signal that his wash had been completed. He sprang to his feet and exited the room while telling us not to move, which we couldn't because we had hardly begun our Martinis, and they are sacred to Harry.

'Where are you leading us, Lottie?' he asked in a whisper, looking round as if he suspected the room was bugged.

'How do I know? Your go next, Mr Harry Writer.'

'Thanks, Lottie.'

'Busk it,' I suggested.

'*Cahiers du Cinéma* indeed—'

'You got us into this job with the washing thing. I mean that got us the job, your sympathy about the washing.'

Before Harry could defend himself Mr Hunter came back into the room looking as if his editing suite had blown up.

'Disaster, disaster!'

He sat down very suddenly opposite us and drank deeply of his Martini.

We waited, somehow knowing that it had to be something to do with washing.

'Hortense has just given in her notice – that I could take – but her parting revenge for Waterloo was to put a tiny yellow duster in the washing machine! All my smalls from the Rue de Rivoli – ruined.'

We stared at him, both of us struggling with our emotions.

'Mr Hunter, if this weren't so tragic it would be *farcical*,' Harry said, eventually, straight-faced. 'In which case you could always tell everyone your smalls were from the Rue *Feydeau*.'

He was not usually in the habit of making heavy-handed jokes about French playwrights, but things were getting so desperate we had to have an excuse to laugh.

Mr Hunter, who had just taken far too big a sip of his dry Martini, made a noise that was somewhere between a snort and a gasp of laughter.

'From now on,' he said finally, 'that is going to be *my* line. I should warn you that anything, but anything, you say in here that is either clever or witty is mine because I am paying you, Mr Harry Writer.'

Even so he was still so distressed about his smalls that his concentration was gone, so we left him shortly afterwards.

Once we were clear of the Hunter mansion we retired to our favourite coffee bar. Since we still had not got any further with the so-called comedy set in Paris that we were meant to be writing, I relented and told Harry about my Rolls-Royce idea. He groaned. Harry's groan was someone else's thumbs down.

'Times are desperate,' I reminded him. 'We have a contract. Besides I want a motor car.'

'Why can't you want a car like everyone else?'

'I like saying motor car. It makes a car sound more important, if you know what I mean?'

'No,' Harry said, and since he was in that kind of mood I left off talking about *Merrily It Rolls Along* and let him stare out of the window in a blue funk. Because that is the best thing to do when you are writing with someone else, leave them alone in their funk. After quite a boring fifteen minutes I left him and went back to Dingley Dell where I had a laugh with Hal and Melville, both sitting up late with my father's whisky, moaning about theatre. I loved to sit listening to actors moaning. I found it very sooth-ing, and of course they were very sympathetic about

Merrily and Mr Hunter, and even thought he would like it.

'Rolls-Royce and Paris? He will bite at it, darling, bite at it,' Hal boomed.

I knew he was just being kind, but as pressures increased and my motor car seemed to be fast disappearing down a minor road never to be seen again, I felt something had to be done, or rather said. We couldn't just sit about and drink Martinis and talk about Mr Hunter's yellow smalls.

I was not wrong. The next evening Mr Hunter was waiting for us with the expectant air of a father-to-be. I avoided looking at him too closely because I knew there was a danger that I would picture him wearing yellow undies under his clothes. Harry poured the Martinis as usual, and to my astonishment began to expound on my idea, avoiding using my title, which I knew he particularly disliked – and no one could blame him.

Mr Hunter was immediately intrigued.

'My dear Lottie, this is just up our Parisian street, would you not say? How clever is Mr Harry Writer?'

I smiled weakly, before giving Harry my 'I'll see you later' look. He smiled back, but his smile had a shrug in it, and his eyes said 'desperate times', and he made a very soft 'vroom-vroom' sound as Mr Hunter walked up and down his drawing room, lighting a cigar and talking about the Rue de Rivoli and Maxim's and the marvels of eating in Paris.

'So this young man answers the advertisement for a chauffeur and takes the old lady to Paris, and she eventually returns to America where she dies, leaving him the Rolls —' He stopped abruptly. 'Was this the way you got your Rolls?' he asked, pointing his cigar at Harry.

Harry opened his mouth to say 'no, actually' or something similar, but I butted in before he could.

'We never discuss the Rolls, Mr Hunter,' I said. 'Never, ever discuss the provenance of a Rolls, or it will immediately lose its magic.'

Harry stared at me as Mr Hunter smiled and then sighed with pleasure. 'My dear Lottie, I like your style. I have liked your style from the moment you came for an interview. Both of you, you have style. And what is more you were the only ******* writers who made me ******* laugh.'

Harry had stopped looking astonished so we were able to continue with the storyline, or 'weenie' as I still insisted we called it, to which I was pleased to say Mr Hunter also adhered.

'So we have Paris, we have a Rolls-Royce, and we have a penniless young man. Now we need another female – not just the old lady.'

'The wise old lady,' I corrected him. 'She is brilliant with stocks and shares. She teaches him how to play the market. Buy low, sell high … you know the kind of thing, Mr Hunter?'

It was something I had heard one of my father's agents say. Needless to say he was very rich and always trying to get my father to follow his example and play the stock exchange, but money was never of interest to my father. He only cared about matters of National Importance, and if my mother ever reminded him that money did not grow on trees he would stare at her in such a way as to suggest that if it didn't – it should.

'So who are we going to for the chauffeur? Burt or Cary? Cary?Yes, Cary. I know them both so well, I have their shoe sizes on file, the kind of chocolate cake that Burty likes, the kind of steak Cary goes for. Oh, yes, they will love this. But what about the girl? Sophia perhaps? Vivien certainly. Although she is now more woman than girl. She has such style, such style! And certainly convinced as Cleopatra …'

'We will leave the casting to you, Mr Hunter. We will just write.'

'You will not just write, my dear Lottie, you will deliver me this script in the next fortnight. And not a day later.'

Mr Hunter's indulgent tone had changed to that of a hardened producer. We quickly drained our Martinis and sprang up.

'See you in fourteen days, Mr Hunter.'

'The bell has rung. It will be your driver.'

We hurried to the front door feeling that even the time it took to get through the hall would be time away from writing the script.

'Did you tell Monty to call for us?'

'Naturally. Have to play the game with the Mr Hunters of this world, Lottie.'

'You might have told me. I didn't think you even liked the idea – didn't like *Merrily*.'

'I don't like the idea. I hate it,' Harry agreed as we settled into the back of Rollo. 'But you want a *motor car* – needs must, Lottie-bags.'

I stared out of the window. Everything always looked so different when we were in Rollo – trees and buses and even London taxis seemed to take on a sheen.

'Do you really think we will get to the end of this script and it will go into production?' I asked Harry later.

He looked up from his typewriter as I looked down at my notes, which were as usual unintelligible.

'I can't even believe we have got this far, Lottie.'

We had barely drafted a word when Mr Hunter started to telephone us. 'Dewi should never have given him my number,' Harry moaned.

Night after night we sat up with that script, and night after night – sometimes at three in the morning – Mr Hunter rang Harry.

Once his washing was done he had great trouble sleeping and it was soon apparent that he was determined that we should have the same problem.

Into the second week Commander Steerforth started to look worried. 'You're looking quite pallid, Lottie.'

'You should see Harry,' I said briefly.

At last the first draft was finished, one week and six days later.

I thought I might have a headache coming on so Harry took it into the Hunter mansion.

When he finally came back and we met in the coffee bar, I stared at him wordless, not because Mr Hunter hated it, but because Harry reminded me of someone, and I now knew who it was. It was the man I had seen coming out of the producer's office what seemed like a lifetime ago.

Of course, I said nothing because I only had to tell Harry that a shirt didn't suit him for him to take to his bed.

'So – the Hunter verdict?'

'He hates it. Too much dialogue, too little sex.'

'Same old, same old,' I said with some relief, thinking that although I would never get my motor car I could at least get some sleep – oh, and Harry too, of course. 'So that is that,' I added, looking round to order some more coffee as a sort of muted celebration.

'No, Lottie, that is not that at all.'

'It must be. The two weeks is over.'

Harry stood up.

'No time for coffee, we have another commission – at least, you have.'

I could feel myself paling. No, really, pale to the lips, white to the gills.

'Burt is coming over, touching down tonight. Mr Hunter wants his dear Lottie to make him a chocolate cake just like she made for Mr Hunter himself.'

'That wasn't my cake, that was one Mrs Graham made for me to take him. I can't ask her to make another. She's got so much on.'

'But you can, Lottie-bags, because on it depends much. Anyway you never told me you left him a cake. Kind of creepy, wasn't it?'

'Yup,' I agreed, miserably. 'It was when Hortense dyed his undies; I thought it might cheer him up between maids.'

'Well, it did cheer him up, and apparently Burty, as Mr Hunter calls him, had a slice or nine and is even now flying back into London with chocolate cake at the top of his dietary requirements. Mr Hunter requests another from his dear Lottie.'

I hurried back to Dingley Dell. Perhaps Mrs Graham would lend me the recipe?

Mrs Graham looked at me.

'You're never going to attempt a cake, Miss Lottie?'

'I am, Mrs Graham,' I said bravely, trying not to see the look on her face.

'Well, take my advice – treble the amounts in the recipe to allow for at least three attempts.'

How I came to hate the sight of chocolate cake, could never be dragged to one of Burt's movies or see the name of Bennett Hunter on a credit without feeling vaguely Uncle Dick, stems from that night.

And the worst of it was that I knew it was entirely my own creepy fault and Harry was quite right not to feel sorry for me.

Monty delivered the final cake in Rollo and reported back that it was received with unconcealed delight, as was Dewi's call shortly after to say that a cheque for the script that Mr Hunter so hated had arrived on his desk.

'I can't understand it,' he said to us over a celebratory lunch. 'Really I can't. Bennett Hunter hated that script, really hated it. It took three calls to tell me just how much. But he still paid you. You know what he kept saying—'

'Too much dialogue, too little sex,' Harry and I both said together before Dewi could go on.

'That's right. Still, now you can get a car.'

'We have one,' we both said again, staring out of the restaurant window at the green Morris Minor parked outside. Dewi stared at where we were looking and tried to look as enthusiastic as we felt.

'It's got imitation leopardskin seats,' I told him proudly.

Dewi gave us both a grave look.

'A very good thing you didn't go up for the Bennett Hunter job in that,' he said, sighing happily. 'Always put on a good show. Or as my mother used to say – never look as poor as you feel.'

A few days later as we walked round to Sunday lunch at Dingley Dell Harry mused as to how or where our script would end up. As a vehicle for some young lovely perhaps? Or maybe an ageing female star would be brought out and dusted down to make a come-back as the old lady who owned the Rolls Royce.

We knew it would probably be some time before we found out the fate of the script, but for the moment the door of Dingley Dell was opening, and the sound of Melville playing Noël Coward's 'I'll See You Again' was drifting towards us. This together with the smell of roast beef cooking was reassuring to say the least.

In the drawing room Hal was arguing with my mother, and my father was pouring drinks. All in all, everything was pretty good in our tiny part of the world, until that is pudding appeared at the lunch table and a glazed look came over my face as my mother announced that my two previous attempts at chocolate cake had gone into Mrs Graham's Sunday trifle.

'You must do this again, Mrs Graham,' Hal boomed at her. 'Chocolate trifle – it's magic.'

Needless to say, Harry promptly hummed a reprise of 'I'll See You Again' as he helped himself to a large spoonful.

Myself, I thought only of the bliss of owning a motor car, and waited for the cheese.

MUCH ADO ABOUT EVERYTHING

Harry was away acting in a film with two very famous British comedians when the telephone on my desk at MI5 rang. It was Dewi and he was sounding excited, which must mean that someone with a leaky Biro had rung him with an idea. In a few seconds this turned out to be true. Apparently the agent of one of the comedians had rung Dewi professing interest in a script that we had written.

'What script is this?' I asked, immediately feeling suspicious, because as far as I knew none of our scripts was worth re-oxygenating.

'*The Happy Communist*,' Dewi answered.

'But that has already been made as *Sexy Aliens*, Dewi. Remember?'

'No, this is the original *Happy Commie*. Apparently Harry gave him the first draft – *The Happy Communist* as you both penned it.'

'But again, it's been paid for under *Sexy Aliens*, Dewi.'

'Back to back, that is the new thing with scripts for films, Lottie, back to back – and inside out too. You film it at the same time using two different scripts, same actors, same director. Cheaper.'

I was always uneasy when Dewi was at his most confident. Besides, *The Happy Communist* had been about a young man like Harry – tall, slim and not a month over twenty-five. Both the very famous comedians were short and tipping into forty, and that was just their waistlines.

At Harry's flat later that day I managed to look reproachful.

'You gave Leslie Johns *The Happy Communist* without telling me,' I stated.

'I did,' Harry agreed as he chopped onions to make us his favourite curry.

'Why this sudden treachery, Harry?'

He smiled as tears from the onions trickled from his eyes.

'Look,' he said, pointing to his face. 'The masks of tragedy and comedy in one,' he said proudly.

'Never mind that,' I said, sticking a piece of bread in his mouth – something Mrs Graham always did when chopping onions. 'Leslie Johns is no more suitable for *The Happy Communist* than Bennett Hunter would be.'

'Oh, I don't know,' Harry replied, throwing the piece of bread over his shoulder. 'Mr Hunter could be magic. Anyway, like it or lump it, Lottie-bags, we meet with the great man when shooting is over.'

That was the trouble with Harry. Like my great-aunt Bibby's pugs, he just didn't do telling off. Pugs did what they did and that was that, and Harry was the same.

I put the matter out of my mind, thinking nothing would come of it.

Besides, there were new challenges for Harry on the horizon, and for me too. We had been asked to contribute to a musical revue, and what's more Harry was to star in it. I had never written sketches before but Harry had, and so I had to learn that a sketch was a little play, which had to have a beginning and a middle and an end, but instead of lasting an hour and a half it took six or seven minutes.

To my astonishment one of my sketches was included in the show. It was particularly astonishing since the main player in the sketch was a tank, which would shoot stars instead of bullets. Needless to say, the sketch was anti-war.

I kept away from rehearsals because Harry told me, quite firmly, that actors hated writers and anyway he was there so he would look after my work.

Of course, I believed him, and besides I was at MI5 during the day, and we were all getting a bit excited because Commander Steerforth and I thought we might have caught a double agent. He was an utterly believable character who could deceive almost anyone – except Commander Steerforth who had a nose for scoundrels due, he said, to having spent so much time at sea.

'The salt breezes clear the nostrils,' he assured me. 'Any nasty tang approaching and you are alerted straight away, and that's without binoculars.'

He was rightly proud of this.

Of course, I could not tell Harry about Commander Steerforth's great catch, but it was one of the reasons that for once my mind was more concentrated on my security work than what was happening in rehearsal.

The opening night was out of town, some way out of town, which made getting there with my parents a bit of a stately progress. My father was looking forward to it because he liked anything with music in it. He did not like straight theatre on the sound principle that the intervals were too long and he did not want to drink himself into the next act. My mother was looking forward to it because although she didn't like musicals, at least revues had sketches. I didn't tell them that I had a sketch in it – I thought it better to keep quiet on that front.

When we arrived I went round to see Harry in his dressing room and he was in a right old state because they hadn't rehearsed enough and there was only one bulb above his mirror, so making up was a nightmare. I did not attempt to calm him – but once again he reminded me of one of Aunt Bibby's pugs. If a pug's tail goes straight he is really in a stew – Harry's tail was straight all right.

So the heavy old-fashioned velvet curtains parted and there was mild applause as a very pretty set was revealed. On came Harry singing, to be joined a few seconds later by a very pretty actress who opened her mouth to respond, only for nothing to come out. The orchestra played on and Harry, obviously loath to be at a complete loss, finally hummed her part obligingly, but still nothing came out of the poor girl's mouth.

'Her jaw's locked,' my mother whispered. My mother knew about these things.

'Harry hums rather well,' my father said, a little too loudly.

The musical number came to an end, to be followed by a sketch set in a restaurant during which Harry had to hurl crockery for reasons I could not quite understand, but I could see that in the process of the hurling he had cut his hand and had to wrap a napkin round it, which worried the audience.

After that things went from worse to much worse as the actress with the locked jaw not only found it hard to sing, but almost impossible to speak, which meant that the other actors were all too often heard to say: 'I think what you mean is ...' The musical numbers continued to be a mess to say the least, with Harry singing as cheerfully as he could only to be responded to by unintelligible responses. Meanwhile the audience went from baffled to hysterical, and the interval was a riot.

I do not like to revel in the misfortunes of others so did not go backstage in the interval but stayed in the bar with my parents, who were looking remarkably relaxed and good-tempered.

'Your mother loves things going wrong – and, I must say, I quite enjoy telling people about it afterwards,' my father murmured. He paused, his expression serious. 'I think Harry is doing splendidly, not easy to hum in tune.'

The curtain rose on the second act of the entertainment and the understudy came on to replace the poor lockjawed lead. She could sing and she could certainly speak, but the truth was that after the excitements of the first act the audience seemed to be waiting for more of the same.

My sketch was the last item of the evening. On came Harry all ready to start the sketch, but the stage manager must have forgotten to do something essential because the tank started to take on a life of its own, making its inexorable way towards the orchestra pit. Harry rushed forward to wedge his foot behind a wheel, while the understudy somehow triggered the device to shoot the stars, which all promptly fell on to the stage. At a screeched command from Harry the poor benighted actress took over from him, wedging her foot under a wheel, while Harry rushed about the stage stamping on the burning stars.

The audience rocked with laughter, the tank was removed, and the revue finally finished with all the cast on-stage singing a rousing number, the words of which I have happily forgotten. But I have an awful feeling they involved everyone having been at a marvellous party.

'I am quite sure your number made the evening for everyone, Lottie,' my father said, patting me on the shoulder when we got back to Dingley Dell.

Harry could not agree. In fact, he could not wait to come off tour and abandon the revue but it staggered on for some months, during which my belief in MI5 grew ever stronger because we caught not one double agent, but two, which made Commander Steerforth as happy as we had ever seen him, if not Monty. To his dismay the Commander's euphoria translated into yet more bouquets for Arabella's mother, and yet more vases to be filled by Monty.

'Say what you like but you can go off flowers, you know,' he kept murmuring every time Arabella and I stopped by.

All in all, it was quite a relief when Harry's revue finally folded, and the poor young leading lady went off in search of a cure for her first-night lockjaw.

I didn't tell Harry but I had become somewhat disillusioned with theatre.

It was so unglamorous backstage, and no one was very happy until they got to the pub afterwards when they all seemed to cheer up like there was no tomorrow.

Harry swore he would never do another revue, which was only understandable.

His thoughts therefore turned to *The Happy Communist*.

'Not the version with Leslie Johns? Please, Harry. Please, please, please.'

He gave me the look he had adopted since my tank sketch. The look said: 'After what you put me through with your sketch, you owe me far too much to argue with me.' And of course I did feel a mountain of guilt about it, so I shut up, which was hard for me.

A bit like the tank rolling inexorably towards the orchestra pit, the whole thing seemed to be trundling on of its own accord, no matter what I thought or felt. Leslie Johns' agent had rung Dewi and they had arranged for us to see him in cabaret at a theatre that seated hundreds more than the usual places where cabaret played.

The evening loomed over me long before it happened. After the revue experience I had developed a fear of anything in the way of live singing and dancing, not to mention comedy. But I didn't want to let Harry down.

The evening started off with Leslie Johns sending a car for us. Well, it wasn't just a car; it was a Bentley, complete with driver. Since it had been sent to Harry's address in downtown Earls Court it drew quite a crowd, I can tell you.

Dermot pointed out of the window at it as we bustled about ready to leave. 'That car cost as much as this flat,' he called after us.

'Get into Variety and you could have both, Dermot,' Harry called back.

He explained to me that it was as necessary to Leslie Johns to put on a good show for us as it had been for us to appear swanky and successful before Bennett Hunter. In fact, it was even more important if you were a Variety star like Leslie Johns because everyone thought you were on the downslide if you didn't turn up in a Rolls-Royce or a Bentley. Their agents couldn't even negotiate if they didn't have a Rolls or a Bentley, not to mention a large house with a swimming pool.

'It's a different world to the theatre, Lottie-bags, quite different. Theatre is small change compared to Variety. Seaside audiences just don't want to see *King Lear* after a shrimp tea and four glasses of Tizer.'

I could understand that, but at the same time I still felt that we might not be the right writers for Leslie Johns.

The memory of the tank incident acted as a dreadful warning.

The evening began with a great many bad acts meant to make the audience restless for the main course, which was of course Leslie Johns.

When he came on he was received with rapture, and understandably so since he gave them what they loved. Nothing entirely new, nothing too dated, just pure Leslie Johns. Harry was thrilled. He loved comedians and often went to see his favourites, never tiring of their catchphrases. I must say I did become a fan of Leslie Johns during the evening, but was still filled with doubt about whether our pens would suit him. One thing I did know was that I would not be putting him in a tank.

'Come on, we're invited backstage,' Harry called to me afterwards.

'Are you sure?'

'Of course I'm sure. It's a rule. You get comps, you go back and thank.'

'We could write a note,' I suggested, following him.

'What – while we're sitting in the back of his car with him?'

Knowing nothing about Variety, I feared I might stick out like a sore thumb at a piano recital or maybe get lockjaw like the poor actress in the revue.

The moment we were shown to Leslie Johns' dressing room with the glittering star on its door and heard the rumble of talk and laughter, I started to feel like I was walking into a new world, which of course I was.

The door was opened by a smart dresser with a bright Hollywood smile.

Behind him a table was set with champagne glasses and not one but two buckets with champagne bottles peeping merrily out of them. The lighting was what Melville would call 'divine'. It was all so different from 'theatre' where the dressing-room lighting was more often than not a row of light bulbs burning forlornly around shabby mirrors. In this dressing room there were no worn-down make-up sticks or frayed towels. This room blazed with light, and to my delighted eyes everyone seemed to be sprinkled with stardust.

Leslie Johns stood in the middle in a wonderful white towelling dressing gown such as champion boxers wear. In his hand, and indeed everyone else's, was a champagne glass, which his circling dresser was busy keeping filled.

Soon Harry and I too had champagne glasses being refilled after every sip. It was a dizzying change after the tooth mugs and cooking sherry that was our normal fayre when visiting friends backstage.

I soon found myself being introduced to Lonny Langley – catchphrase 'Getting along with Lonny, incher?' I knew him from watching Sunday telly with my father who was a Lonny Langley fan.

'I have heard a great deal about you young writers,' he said, smiling widely.

'If that is the case perhaps I had better go?' I quipped. Valiantly – or lamely, depending on how you view such an answer. 'Although we have written a film for Bennett Hunter but – it hasn't been oxygenated yet.'

He purred.

'I can see why Leslie has his eye on you,' he stated, getting closer and closer to me.

'Really?'

'You know who I am, of course?'

'Yes, of course. You are very, very famous.'

'Yes, I am,' he agreed.

'You are almost as famous as the Queen.'

'Almost.' He puffed on his long diamanté-encrusted cigarette holder. 'And almost as rich. Although her tiara is bigger than mine, something I will have fixed before my next panto. People …' he confided, realising that I was riveted, and anyway he was so close to me, I could not move even if I'd wanted to. 'People,' he went on, 'many, many people, keep trying to make me ashamed of my success, but I refuse to be. I will not be ashamed of my Rolls-Royce, or my villa in the South of France, or my penthouse in Brighton, or my flat in Belgravia. I am proud to be successful. In this country, too many people are cut down to size because of their success. I say: more. More success is what I work for – just like the Queen.'

As he was speaking Lonny Langley advanced closer and closer to me, which meant that I stepped further and further back and back until I ended up against the wall, my eyes popping out of my head because I had never before been privileged to hear a monologue like this. It was both exciting, and strangely subversive.

Money was never talked about at Dingley Dell and with good reason; there was not enough of it about to support a conversation of any lasting interest.

'I am very, very jealous of Leslie employing you, very jell-jell indeed.'

'Oh, I shouldn't be,' I reassured him. 'We are—'

I was about to embark on a modest speech about only just beginning when I realised that it would be against his principles, so I stopped.

'You are?'

'Only passing brilliant.'

'There you go again!' He laughed immoderately. Then he leaned forward and whispered in my ear, 'Have you ever done panto?'

'Not as such.'

'But you would love to, of course?'

'Of course.'

'Your agent shall be notified by my agent.'

He went to move away as he saw Leslie Johns bearing down on us.

'But, hush, here comes the wicked Baron.'

Soon afterwards the party broke up, and Harry took me firmly by the arm and guided me out of the theatre where we waited for Leslie Johns.

'You want to be careful of Lonny Langley,' Harry said, crossly. 'He has a very bad reputation.'

'What for?'

'What do you think? Pinching—'

'Chorus girls?'

'No, writers,' Harry said, even more crossly.

'He doesn't seem the type, seems the other way,' I said absently.

Leslie Johns came out and we followed him into his Bentley. It was his turn to look at me.

'You want to be careful of Lonny,' he said, sternly.

'I just told her,' Harry said quickly.

'He's always pinching writers.'

I gazed out of the window, not wanting to tell either of them how I felt. I did not mind if Lonny Langley pinched us, or anyone else for that matter. The truth was I had fallen heavily in love with Variety.

*

The following evening at the flat Dermot was much in evidence hanging about where we normally worked, huddled behind a screen for privacy. He kept poking his head round the side to ask unnecessary questions along the lines of, did one of us plan to have a bath tonight?

Harry rolled his eyes at me so much I thought he might pass out with the effort. Finally he got up and beckoned to me to leave.

'We're going to the coffee bar to write, Dermot,' he called. 'It's much quieter.'

I trotted along beside Harry, who was inclined to forget that I was a great deal shorter.

'Dermot,' he explained as I went into an extended trot to keep up, 'overheard our conversation about Leslie Johns and wants to find out whether we're going to take up the offer, because if we don't he will.'

'Coat-tailing as usual,' I muttered.

'It would be easier to write in an Anderson shelter than at the flat.'

I stopped trotting and after a bit Harry did look back and notice.

'I am not handing yet another job to that sneak Dermot, not even if I have to write for both Leslie Johns and Lonny Langley at the same time.'

Harry beckoned me to catch up. 'We are not writing for either of them.'

I stopped again.

'I am,' I said, wearing my best intransigent expression.

'You must be kidding?'

'No, I am not,' I said, firmly, and resumed trotting so quickly that this time Harry had to catch up with me.

'But you didn't even want to see his show … you didn't want to see Leslie Johns' show.'

'I know,' I agreed. 'But that was before I went backstage and saw his dressing room and all that champagne, and those lovely thick white towels.'

'Lottie—'

Since Harry had been left speechless we did not resume our conversation until we had settled into our usual coffee-bar pews.

'Lottie,' Harry said again, louder, because I was busy staring at the menu wondering whether to have chips with my omelette, which was always a difficult moment for me.

I put down the menu.

'It's no good, I will have to have chips.'

'Lottie, we can't write for Variety. We're too finely wrought for that kind of rough and tumble. Do you know what they get up to?'

'Yes, Harry, and I don't care. I want to be in dressing rooms that serve champagne and have performers wearing nice clean dressing gowns and dressers that smile and are charming.'

'What about artistic integrity? Whatever happened to that?'

'It's in the Lost Property Office at Victoria Station. I might pick it up – in a few weeks' time.'

'You don't realise what it's like to write for a comedian.'

'Nor do you.'

'I'm not ringing Dewi.'

'He'll be thrilled.'

I sighed happily. Well, I would. The chips had just arrived.

As it happened Dewi was not as thrilled as we had both imagined he would be.

'Leslie Johns can be tricky, Lottie.'

'There are two of us, Dewi, we should be all right.'

'Depends on what you call all right. Remember Bennett Hunter? That was the only time Harry has ever called me after six.'

'He never told me he called you after six. What about?'

'Ask Harry.'

Dewi put the phone down, but of course I didn't ask Harry, I couldn't – not after the chocolate cake incident. I turned my thoughts to higher things such as Sunday lunch at Dingley Dell, which in recent weeks had become a bit of a bookie's parlour.

Hal and myself, and of course Harry, had all decided to liven things up by coming up with who was the least likely MI5 recruit. Melville was the stakeholder.

I had always understood that if my father had a recruiting principle it was to attract people who were seemingly anonymous.

'Hal and I are some of his exceptions,' Melville stated. 'And Harry, of course – a bit. We are the show business exceptions.'

'I don't suppose he has anyone in Variety working for him,' Harry mused.

'The moment we see someone at the Palladium coming on with the catchphrase "what I couldn't tell you … my lips are sealed", we will know,' Hal boomed.

'I think my money is safe,' Melville said complacently.

All good stuff, as my father would say, but just at that moment Harry and I had been recruited by Leslie Johns and we had to go to work for him straight away as he needed fresh material for his summer show.

Since I was still committed to the service and Commander Steerforth in particular – not to mention Arabella – we went to work for Leslie Johns after I had finished for the day at MI5 and visited him on Saturdays.

Leslie Johns' house was vast, at least by our standards. While Dingley Dell was elegant and old-world faded and gracious to its fingertips, if a house can have fingertips, Leslie Johns' was a bit like his Bentley. It radiated success from every inch of its Tudoresque beams to its impeccably mown lawns.

The door was flung open to us – and I do mean us because Monty had once again insisted that we use Rollo.

'It's not me, it's Mademoiselle,' he said, trying to look innocent, at which he was not at all clever. 'Mademoiselle told me to look after you. Besides, I'm a fan of Leslie Johns.'

'And what Zuzu wants Zuzu gets,' Harry said, sighing.

'Precisely,' Monty said, breathing in and breathing out in that particular way he always did when Zuzu's name was mentioned. It was as if her particular magic made him feel short of breath, which I could understand. Zuzu always left you wondering why everyone else wasn't her, or hoping that if you tried hard you could become more like her. She trailed enchantment in her wake. She could make roses open, stars leave their galaxy to join in the fun; and you always knew where she had been because she would leave a light fragrance of Je Reviens on the air.

Hurry and I were shown into a very large drawing room with not one but two televisions in evidence.

'When I'm on telly I like to see myself double, which I usually do anyway thanks to the dry Martinis,' Leslie quipped as he came into the room.

There was something very endearing about him. He never referred to his hard climb to success or the ghastly days of the war when he was playing the factories with only his old mum in attendance. He left his publicity woman to do that. Leslie seemed merely to take it for granted that everyone in Variety had a stiff climb to the top and they were all the better for it.

'So – where to begin? I love your work.'

Harry and I attempted to smile modestly, and waited.

'I caught the revue you were in,' he went on, speaking to Harry. 'I slipped in and saw the dress rehearsal. That tank sketch was the funniest thing in the show.'

There was the now familiar-to-me sound of Harry's jaw dropping.

'I would certainly like to use that for my summer show. So, what else have you got in the famous pipeline?'

'We have a sketch about a farmer who befriends a pig,' I improvised quickly.

'Do tell,' Leslie said, lighting up a cigar.

'The farmer can't bring himself to send the pig to market so he teaches it to do tricks, one of which is to impersonate him.'

Leslie drew on his cigar.

'I can just see it. I can just see it,' he repeated. 'The pig can keep coming up with my catchphrase all wrong. Once he learns it successfully, I can make the audience honk along. Finally we exit hand in hand, with his trotter in mine. We must get a pig costume made straight away – animal costumiers are notoriously slow. Always some excuse – either they can't get the ears for the rats, or the horses' hooves have to be different sizes. Or the teeth don't fit. Always something, I promise you. I'll order up the pig today.'

I have to tell you, the moment Leslie turned his back Harry gave me a look that would have made a lesser writer break out in a sweat. In return I did what I always do when he does that — I pulled a face. Unfortunately Leslie turned round at just the wrong moment.

'Are you all right?' he asked, quickly blessing himself.

'She always does that when she's happy,' Harry put in quickly.

'I'll know what to look for then.'

'So,' Harry went on. 'You like the pig idea.'

Leslie's face grew serious.

'I don't like it,' he said. 'I adore it. I knew you were the writers for me when I saw the tank sketch in rehearsal. Just knew it.'

It was soon incumbent on Harry to come up with some more ideas because I was exhausted by my own brilliance, as I often was. It meant I had to go into a minute's trance from which I returned with reluctance.

When I did return Harry had come up with two other ideas for sketches, if not three other ideas, and it was Leslie's turn to go into a trance-like state, sighing as he did so before ringing for champagne.

'How did it go?' Monty asked as he drove us back to ordinary life.

'Brilliantly,' Harry responded before turning to me. 'You're doing the pig sketch,' he said firmly. 'I'm having nothing to do with it.'

'It was a good thing he only caught the dress rehearsal of the tank sketch, wasn't it? I mean before Debbie's lockjaw set in.'

'Depends on what you call a good thing,' Harry said gloomily.

I left him at the flat and went back to Dingley Dell because I could see he was about to get an attack of 'should we be doing this sort of work?' which in the past has always led to him suggesting that I should read Bernard Shaw's Prefaces, or Proust in the French, which of course I intended to do when I had finished being a writer. I mean you have to spend your time advisedly when you're writing. Keep away from brilliant minds or they put you off your stroke.

Very soon, to everyone's astonishment, Leslie Johns had a clutch of sketches for his summer season show. And even the pig costume was on its way.

The opening night was hugely attended. Happily for the management, it was pouring with rain so no one wanted to linger on the beach or the seafront, which meant that they had a shoal of last-minute bookings.

From the moment the show started it was a success. It might be that the holidaying audience were easily pleased, but the moment Leslie Johns strolled on-stage, his trademark top hat placed at a rakish angle, the audience adored him. This was not such a surprise since they already did, but the truth was he was magnificent. He had a stage presence that hardly needed lighting.

By the interval Harry had turned from being an admirer to an adoring fan.

'He played the audience like an old Joanna,' he said. 'So relaxed, so in touch with them. He makes everyone feel as if he is playing just to them. He is brilliant – quite brilliant.'

The curtains closed, the show ended and we joined the queue outside Leslie's vast dressing room. Once again it was filled with happy faces drinking champagne.

Harry was visibly flattered when Leslie asked us to stay behind when the rest of the crowd had gone.

'At least half of this show's triumph is due to your work,' he said. 'Thanks to you the evening never sags. There are no "once this is over we'll get to the good bit" moments.'

We both looked suitably modest, which actually we felt. Especially me since Harry's sketches were actually better than mine, and less heavy on props.

'Leslie, you are a genius, but then you know that,' Harry told him, and we both raised our glasses to him. 'What you do is far harder than anything a theatrical knight does. They have a genius called Shakespeare to support them. You only have yourself and scribblers like us. You are brilliant. And as I say – so relaxed.'

Leslie smiled and slowly, carefully, put his champagne glass down. 'My dears, let me show you the price of relaxation,' he said, and opened his hands.

His dresser nodded at them. 'And his feet aren't that much better, are they dear?' he said. Harry and I fell silent for a second. We were not just star-struck, we were awestruck. So that was what it took to be that relaxed?

It was always difficult to go back to real life after being in a Variety star's dressing room, but the fact was we had other commitments.

MI5 was on full alert. Commander Steerforth was on brilliant form, and hot on the scent of yet another double agent. This was always exciting, but it did make Arabella a bit jealous as her boss was only a foot follower when it came to netting agents. She made up for it by going for night classes in hieroglyphics

'Why hieroglyphics?'

'Because I want to visit the Pharaohs' tombs and read the walls without a guide telling me all wrong. You know, the Egyptians were a great people. If their dog died they would cover themselves with black ashes and their household furniture in black cloths. The mourning went on for days on end.'

Following this information we both fell into a reverential silence because both Arabella and I worshipped dogs.

'Elgar had special chairs for his dogs,' she continued. 'No one was allowed to sit on their cushions without his permission.'

I nodded. I worshipped Elgar too.

'And Kipling, he was the same about dogs. And of course there's Byron's "Epitaph" to his Newfoundland—'

Before she could delve any further into writers who loved dogs, I unwrapped a small parcel.

'How strange we should be talking about this again,' I said, handing her a book and a badge. 'I have enrolled us both in the Dog Spotters Club. You get a badge too.'

Arabella sighed happily.

'This will make walking across Green Park even more exciting,' she said happily.

It was not the only excitement in my life. Melville was still running a book on one of us being able to spot my father's least likely agent. It was driving Harry mad. He wanted to win so much.

'The little lady who comes up from the country with the home-made marmalade—'

'Everyone knows her,' I said in disparaging tones.

'The window cleaner with the eyepatch he keeps changing from eye to eye.'

'Harry, he's been an agent from the beginning of time. You are hopeless at this, you're never going to win the money.'

Nothing made him more determined than being told he was not going to win. A few weeks went by and then I bumped into Melville on the stairs.

'You'll never believe this, Lottie.'

'What is it I will never believe, Melville?'

'Harry has won the five pounds for agent spotting. I coughed up straight away. No one will be able to top this.'

'You're jolly joking!'

'I am not jolly joking, Lottie.'

'Tell me! Tell me quick as you can before I pass out.'

We both sat down on the stairs, which is something Melville and I do when we are exchanging confidences.

'Yes, Harry only got it in one. Telephoned me just now.'

'Go on, I am in very long suspenders.'

Melville lowered his voice to a whisper. 'It's Lonny Langley.'

I stood up and then sat down again.

'Is there no one who doesn't work for my father?'

'Probably not.'

Now we were both whispering. Well, hissing is probably a better word. 'So how did Harry find out?'

'Apparently it was when he went to meet your father on spooky business, and realised he used Lonny's catchphrase. 'Passed Me By It Did' as his password. Perfect really.'

My mouth fell open, which was never attractive as Melville promptly told me. Everything was falling into place. Now I realised why my father so enjoyed Leslie Langley on the telly. Perhaps even some of his sketches were coded messages? Anything was possible.

'Anyway happy endings all round. Harry has given the money back. I am to donate his winnings to the Actors' Benevolent Fund.'

I felt very proud of Harry for lots of reasons, so when I met him that night in the coffee bar I bought him a spaghetti Bolognese.

We neither of us talked about why. We both knew.

That's partnership for you. Knowing.

STAIRWAY TO THE STARS

Bennett Hunter had been our first major experience of film writing, and as far as I was concerned, what with the chocolate cake-making and Harry getting in a stew and having to ring Dewi in the middle of the night, it was probably going to be our last. For some reason every writer we knew longed to work in films. I was not one of them.

Harry felt differently. He considered our experience with Mr Hunter to have been not as bad as I remembered it, but then he had not had to make three chocolate cakes in order to reach the kind of perfection needed to thrill Mr Hunter's terribly famous movie star.

As it happened I need not have worried about film work as there was a lull in interest in our writing. Happily, this did not affect Harry's acting work. Far from it. A great many people were interested in his acting, so much so that it was difficult for him to know in which direction he should be going. All in all, this meant our writing partnership would be going on hold until after such time as Harry had decided which offer to take up. Many evenings of agonising went on at the coffee bar. I was all for him continuing to act in roles that paid, but Harry wanted to do something artistic rather than successful, so he finally chose to do a play by an unknown French playwright.

'It's a Mackintosh part,' Melville said after he had read the play with waning interest. 'Young actors love them.'

Since it was about a tramp who had stepped off a train at the wrong station, I did not invite my parents because it wasn't a musical and plays about tramps were the sort of thing that made my mother long for *Hamlet*. Harry's parents declined for the sound excuse that they were on a golfing holiday.

The first night was sparsely attended by civilians, just a few critics and people related to the cast, all of whom, after the curtains closed, quickly disappeared into the night looking bewildered.

'What was happening out there?' Harry demanded when I went backstage afterwards.

'Lots of sleeping.'

He was puzzled. He really believed in the play and couldn't understand why the audience found it boring.

'They don't understand the philosophy behind it; they're just not getting the metaphor.'

'As far as those poor souls were concerned it might as well have been in semaphore,' I said, sighing.

'We have to have something besides Shakespeare and Noël Coward in modern theatre.'

'Yes – but perhaps not this.'

Harry was disappointed in me. He had worked hard to make the tramp a fully rounded human being, and to give him his due had done a good job; the trouble was that the tramp only seemed to want to talk about himself, and since the next train never arrived the audience became as irritated as a bunch of commuters who'd just been told there were leaves on the line. A suicide might have woken them up.

Hal and Melville, to their great credit, came to a performance. They were sympathetic and kindly, but Hal was immediately into finger-wagging.

'If this is the kind of play managements are putting on then I have no idea where theatre is going,' he boomed.

'I think there is room in the theatre for this sort of experimental play, Hal,' Harry ventured.

'There was certainly room in the stalls tonight!' Hal boomed.

I am sorry to say that we all found this very funny – although not Harry, of course. Hal and Melville left us to go to their club while Harry and I walked home, because funds were running low and our motor car was in the garage for repairs. Besides, it gave us time to talk over our problems, which were mainly to do with the direction we should be taking.

'We must make a plan,' Harry kept insisting.

'Show business isn't about planning. Show business is like buses: the right one comes along and you get on it, or you don't.'

Harry stopped walking.

'Now you understand the play! That is exactly what it's about.'

'In that case, the playwright should have made his point better,' I said, before making a mental note to call Dewi in the morning when I got to MI5.

'There's not much going on, Lottie,' Dewi told me, sighing when he heard my voice. 'Leslie Johns is having a great time with your sketches. I went to see the show last night and there were any number of people tearing up the place – they loved it.'

I looked across my desk at Arabella who as usual was looking wise. 'Lunch at Fenwick's?' she asked.

Arabella was the kind of friend who just knew when you were in desperate need of egg mayonnaise.

'You're pulling in opposite directions,' she said, stating the obvious, but it was good to hear it said out aloud. 'Harry wants to starve for Art and you just want to get on with everything.'

'Exactly,' I said, but only once I had finished the egg mayonnaise. Arabella looked mystical.

'Something will happen,' she said, finally.

'I hope so.'

'It always does. Look at what happened to the Egyptians.'

I knew what she meant, but I wasn't sure that I wanted to end up in a tomb alongside a pharaoh, however handsome.

'Some day my pharaoh will come,' I sang on the way back to the office, but Arabella wasn't listening. She was too immersed in her *How to Read Hieroglyphics* book.

I knew Arabella well enough to take her predictions seriously. She had said something would happen, so I was not surprised when, only a few days later, the telephone on my desk rang. It was Dewi, and he was not just excited. He was over-excited.

'Lottie! You know I was in to see Leslie Johns' summer show recently? Well, I never told you, but Charles Zuckerman and his entourage were in too.'

'Oh, good.'

'Not good, Lottie ... incredible, because – wait for it – he laughed from start to finish, most particularly at your sketches and Harry's. I know because I had my glasses trained on him all the time. So I bumped into him in the intervals several times and made myself very known to him. He's over here looking for writers to take back with him for his television shows, and he wants you and Harry to go over and see him at Claridge's.'

'What does he want us for?'

'Writing, Lottie. He wants you and Harry to join his team of writers. He thinks your sketches are pure gold.'

'Have you told Harry?'

'No. But I shall.'

'No, don't, I'll tell him. You make the date.'

Harry was still in doleful mood after his Mackintosh part, so I thought I would surprise him about going to meet Charles Zuckerman. Before I did, though, I would confide in Commander Steerforth.

'Oh, I shouldn't do that, Lottie. Really I shouldn't. Men only like to be surprised by a cheque. Going about their day-to-day business they hate surprises. Surprises always find you in the wrong shoes.'

I knew what he meant. A friend of mine never got over a surprise birthday party her husband threw for her because she hadn't had her hair done. You can see her point.

I was in a quandary. If I told Harry in his present mood that he was going to be interviewed by Charles Zuckerman, he would give me his 'you are a bloated capitalist' look and refuse to escort me through the hallowed doors of Claridge's.

I went back to sitting on the stairs with Melville. 'Come up one step,' he ordered.

'Why?'

'You're on the blank thoughts step. You don't want that.'

Melville was right. If my blank thoughts were cheques, I'd be Charles Zuckerman.

'What is your problem, Lottie?'

I told him about Charles Zuckerman and knowing that Harry would never go up for the job if it was served to him straight.

'Best to keep a good writer's distance between you and that, Lottie,' Melville said, putting on his about-to-have-great-thoughts expression. 'Ask Gus what to do, and he can have a confidential talk with Dewi, and between them they will come up with something. But they mustn't tell you or that will be the end of everything.'

I did as Melville advised, and then I tried not to think about what might happen next. It was very difficult. I had to stay away from both agents; plans might be being hatched. I could hardly sleep for worrying. After all, as Dewi had said, Mr Zuckerman was not just big – he was huge.

Commander Steerforth realised that all was not well. 'You're looking peaky again, Lottie.'

I nodded sadly.

'I'm feeling peaky, Commander.'

'It will all sort itself out.'

'We've only got a few days for that to happen.'

'Take some dictation – that will lift your spirits.'

It didn't, of course, but his concern was touching, to say the least. I went home on the bus that evening not expecting much more from life beyond dog-spotting and the occasional lunch at Fenwick's.

Round at the flat Dermot opened the door. He nodded towards our writing screen.

'He's behind that and he's drinking,' he said, darkly.

I peered round the screen. Harry embraced me.

'You'll never guess,' he said. 'Dewi telephoned and you will not believe this – the great Charles Zuckerman wants to see us, tomorrow evening.'

I did not have to act stunned, I was stunned. 'Tomorrow evening?'

'Yes. Now wait for it. He is a huge fan of—'

'Our work?'

'Oh, yes, yes, of course that too, but more than that—'

'He saw the Mackintosh play?'

'Exactly right. At any rate, Charles Zuckerman thinks it is a masterpiece. So, you see, I was not wrong to do that play, Lottie-bags. I am not alone in recognising genius. I feel so vindicated! And tomorrow we will meet this man of great taste. Although why he should want to see us, I don't know.'

We had a drink or three and I returned to Dingley Dell with a renewed respect for agents and their wiles, and when I told Melville that I had acted on his advice and it had all seemingly come right, he was justifiably proud.

*

The following evening as Monty parked Rollo outside Claridge's, the doormen sprang to so quickly it was as if they already knew we were coming. We had hardly said our names before we were immediately shown up to Mr Zuckerman's suite. Inside there was a coal fire burning in the elegant hall. The doors of the drawing room were opened wide and we were announced.

Mr Zuckerman was immediately affable. If you can exude an aura of affability, he did. He was rounded but not fat, smartly and expensively dressed, and smoking the inevitable cigar. He moved towards us with his right hand outstretched, and as he did so the people by whom he was surrounded seemed to be moving with him as if he had contained them in his own magic circle, an unseen force from which they could not escape.

'How marvellous to see you,' he said. 'I love your work. Just love it.'

At the mention of our work my toes moved into scrunch position. Oh, please help him to stick to our work, and not mention the blasted French play. It might be the end of everything.

I glanced at Harry, hoping against hope that he would not pitch straight into some great speech about the tramp on the station platform and the metaphor and all that, but Mr Zuckerman did not give him the time. He straight away offered a cigar, which to my astonishment

Harry accepted. The cigar was so big that he could hardly close his mouth around it. When he could, Mr Zuckerman's assistant promptly lit it. Cigars were truly not Harry, probably because they interrupted him. Besides, as he later confessed, after only a few puffs, they made him feel sick.

I quickly saw that it would be up to me to agree with everything Mr Zuckerman said, and he said a great deal. Among other things he wanted us to come to America and join his team of writers in Hollywood. He would fly us out there courtesy of the television company.

'America will suit you,' he said firmly. 'You're young and zippy and talented – that is the stuff of Hollywood. You will join our team.'

I glanced at Harry, but he was still valiantly puffing, so I pitched in. 'That's very kind of you, but we're a partnership, Mr Zuckerman,' I told him firmly. 'We don't do team work. It is just how it is.'

I did not look at Harry as I spoke. Principally because I thought, what with the heat in the room and the cigar he might be about to take an early exit.

Mr Zuckerman put his head on one side.

'So,' he said, glancing round the room at his entourage. 'Here we have a young lady who still has a long plait of brown hair down her back and is barely out of college, I would say, and she is telling me – the great Charles Zuckerman – how she works.'

The faces in his inner circle were frozen in varying expressions. Only one winked at me. I made a note of him, just in case we ever got to America which I very much doubted.

'It is best to lay out our terms at the outset, don't you think, Mr Zuckerman?'

Charles Zuckerman stared at me.

'Well, yes, I do, young lady. I do think that.' He started to laugh. 'Well, aren't you the darnedest?' he asked me.

'Possibly if not absolutely,' I agreed.

By this time Harry had taken the cigar out of his mouth so the steam-engine effect was less in evidence.

'My partner speaks for us both, Mr Zuckerman,' he stated.

'You Limeys, anyone would think you won the war! Let me tell you about our shows and what material we will be looking for. Original, funny obviously – and American. Do you write American?'

At that moment I would have written in Lithuanian.

'I have relatives in America,' Harry said with some truth. 'We can write it, and even speak it too – when necessary. We like writing American.'

'We were brought up on American television shows – *Bilko* and *I Love Lucy,* you know – all those,' I put in.

Charles Zuckerman glanced around.

'How about these kids?' he asked. 'We've got to take them with us, haven't we?'

They all murmured 'sure thing', or at least that is how I heard it.

The young man with the wink did it again, so I thought it all right to smile at him.

'Enough said.' Mr Zuckerman shook our hands.

We said thank you rather too much and shook everyone else's hands. 'We fly out tomorrow. See you in New York, and then on to Hollywood.'

Harry and I left. In the lift he considered the cigar.

'I'm never sure whether to leave the band on or not — it's the sort of thing my father just knows,' he moaned, staring at it as if it was a hand grenade.

When we reached the ground floor we made our way to the revolving door feeling as if we had just passed our driving tests.

'You're on your way now,' Monty called back to us as he drove us through the Park. 'Once you join the big time at Claridge's the world is definitely at your writing feet.'

'Oh, I don't think anything will come of it, Monty,' Harry said airily. 'Jolly nice of him to see us, but we are not suited to America. We are far, far too English.'

I couldn't have agreed less. I thought going to work in America would be a great experience, so I gazed out of the window and dreamed of walking down Fifth Avenue in a smart new outfit and the kind of high heels that can only be described as cruel.

A few days later I went to see Dewi in his new office.

'You look quite different here,' I announced.

'The rent's much higher,' he said sadly, 'probably because there are less flies. Actually I quite miss their buzzing.'

'And you've got new teacups,' I said brightly because flies are not my subject.

Dewi stared at the cups.

'I dunno who they're from, Lottie, really I don't. They just arrived. I hope I don't get sent a bill because they're a bit floral for me. Can't be from anyone I know. No one I know likes me.'

Of course, they were from me; not really a generous gift, just self-protection, because the old cups were health hazards, what with the chips in the china and handles missing.

'I liked the old ones,' Dewi said sadly. 'They reminded me of the bombing in the war.'

I was getting a little tired of Dewi and his china so I refused a cup of tea and went straight to the subject of our meeting, which was of course Harry.

'He just won't go to America,' I said. 'He thinks writing American jokes would destroy our writing style. And he doesn't want to do that sort of work.'

'What do you think?'

'I love just the thought of America,' I said, sighing. 'Anyway I happen to know that the reason Harry won't go to America is nothing to do with art or writing, but because he won't get on an aeroplane, not at any price.'

Dewi lit a cigarette and looked serious.

'Why don't you leave it to me, Lottie? We've got so far with Mr Zuckerman it seems a shame not to try and get a bit further.'

'How far have you got, Dewi?'

He managed to look mysterious and devious both at the same time, which was almost enviable.

'I have got further than I thought, but not as far as I think I can get,' he said.

And with that I had to be content.

'All this American interest is making you restless instead of happy,' Commander Steerforth stated when I took him some Victoria sponge.

He was right. I knew Harry would never be persuaded to get on a plane, and I knew that the studio would never pay for two scribblers to sail the ocean waves on one of the great liners. As so often happens in show business, I saw the whole excitement slipping away.

I had not counted on Dewi.

Nowadays every afternoon, around sponge-cake time, the telephone on my desk at MI5 rang, and every afternoon there was more transatlantic news that I could not tell Harry.

'I have never known a negotiation like it, Lottie. Each time I tell Mr Zuckerman's people that they are not offering good enough terms they go crazy So far they have offered not just money and a contract; they have offered the best suite in New York's finest hotel. A car to be put at your disposal, to take you out to weekend wherever you want. They just won't take no for an answer. I tell you, Lottie, I am exhausting their impatience.'

'Just a minute – what sort of car, Dewi?' I asked, suddenly alerted to a possible opening with Harry.

'I'll find out.' He paused. 'You know what Richard Burton always says?'

Of course I didn't.

'Apparently he always says that American producers are like randy – sorry, Lottie, but you know what I mean – yes, like randy men. Turning them down only makes them more eager. I know I'm the same – I mean, I was the same, before I met Mrs Dewi.'

I didn't like to think of Dewi having a body, only a desk and a telephone, so I quickly rang off, thinking hard – which always makes my hair go funny.

What I wanted more than anything was to go to the land of the Hershey bar, and movies and jazz and all that.

In the evening I questioned Harry on his favourite makes of car and made a note of one of them before ringing Dewi and telling him to make sure that particular car would be made available to us.

Sad to relate, this did not do it for Harry.

'We now have the best suite at the best hotel, the car at your disposal, the money, everything we asked for. What else can you possibly need, Lottie?' Dewi screamed at me.

'Some wings for Harry to fly the Atlantic,' I said sadly.

Sunday lunch at Dingley Dell was as usual: Melville playing the piano, Hal booming, my mother arguing with him, my father pouring drinks.

This particular Sunday my father beckoned to Harry and me. 'Come into the garden,' he said, using his most confidential tone.

Harry glanced at me. It was not usual for my father to ask us both into the garden, so something must be up.

Harry took a large sip of his drink and so did I. What had we done?

I quickly wondered whether Harry had made a botch of some minor spooky business that my father had sent him on, but then I would not have been beckoned to by the finger.

'You're going to America, I hear.'

'The contract has yet to be signed, sir,' Harry said quickly.

'But it will be,' my father replied with that particular confidence he only employed while intent on getting something wrapped up quickly. 'You'll be on your way to the land of the free. While you are there, I want you to keep eyes and ears open for me … for the service.

We have a long tradition dating to before the war of using people like you to report back on anything you discover that might be of particular interest to us – Noël Coward, Somerset Maugham – we like using creative people, usually writers.'

All the time he was speaking he was only addressing himself to Harry. My mind never really races, but seeing my father concentrating on him in that way, it did start to rev up. Had Melville told my father that Harry was being a stick in the mud about the US of A? Did Dewi work for my father?

This was such a new and unexpected development that I was prepared to believe anything.

'I'm not sure I am up to that kind of work, sir,' Harry said, his voice rising.

'Oh, I think you are, Harry. In fact, I know you are. I will give you more details nearer the time. You will prove very useful to us, I'm sure.'

My father's tone was so final that I could almost see my passport being stamped by American officials.

'You'll do a good job, Harry, and you will serve your country, which I know you are eager to do.'

After that poor Harry could hardly eat his lunch. I wolfed mine. There was no going back now. We would be on our way soon, or so I thought. I'd counted without Harry.

Night after night when we met to work, he sat about moaning that he couldn't get on an aeroplane.

'I don't understand how they stay up,' was his main reason.

'I don't understand how the telephone works, but I still use it.'

'You don't cross the Atlantic on a telephone, Lottie.'

I got to my feet, finally fed up.

'Tell you what, Harry, I'll go without you and you can stay in the flat and phone your jokes in.'

Now he too stood up.

'You are not going to Hollywood on your own. I saw that man in Claridge's winking at you.'

'Winking is not a crime, Harry, but missing opportunities is.'

'Oh, very well, I'll go.'

'I'll ring Dewi and tell him.'

Dewi was pleased, but practical.

'Richard Burton always says just because a woman says yes, you can't always be sure she'll follow through. We may have a "yes" from Harry but we have to get him on the plane, Lottie. That's still ahead of us.'

Happily, Harry's acting agent had a client on his books who specialised in burly-man-in-pub parts and was built accordingly. He was to meet us in the VIP lounge, all part of our contract courtesy of Mr Zuckerman for whom I now had the same admiration as Arabella did for Gandhi.

Once my suitcases were packed and everything at the ready, my parents said goodbye to me with stiff-upper-lip expressions. Hal and Melville lined the hallway to wish me luck and embrace me.

As I was turning to go and get into Rollo where Harry was waiting for me, Melville gave me a small box.

'It's for Harry.'

On the drive to the airport he opened it.

It was a badge with at its centre a winking eye.

Melville's note read: *First prize for agent-spotting, Harry. Wear it with pride.*

Harry pinned it on immediately.

At the airport the burly actor took us to the bar where he poured Martinis down Harry, and then – I kid you not – strong-armed him up the steps of the waiting plane and into his first-class seat.

When the plane took off I could not contain my happiness. We were on our way at last. Everything had fallen into place.

Commander Steerforth had given me leave to take a sabbatical – knowing that we were to be doing undercover work, he patted me on the shoulder and murmured encouraging things. He said he thought I would do a fine job in America because of spying being in my blood, which in a strange way I suppose it is.

Arabella gave me a sacred stone from somewhere holy and Eastern. She didn't tell me where because she knows my geography knowledge stops at the King's Road.

'It will bring you luck.'

As the plane rose into the skies I put my hand into my handbag and took out the little stone.

'Here, hold this,' I said to Harry, but the Martinis seemed to have taken effect because he had fallen fast asleep.

I stared ahead, thinking of that great country the US of A. The country of Lincoln, of Cole Porter, of Duke Ellington ... of practically everyone.

I was going to the place of their birth. In eighteen hours I would be in New York.

But I nearly wasn't.

WELCOME TO AMERICA

Our journey was sybaritic thanks to Pan Am. Comfortable bunks, wonderful food, altogether a dream of luxury travelling, thanks to Mr Zuckerman and the studio.

Harry stepped off the aircraft looking as if it was his birthday, until he faced a customs officer who was not in the best of moods.

'Very well, sir,' he said, having finally checked through everything. 'I need to ask you one more thing … what's that badge you're wearing?'

'This?' Harry answered gaily. 'Oh, this was awarded for being great at spotting spies! It's a British thing!'

'Is that so? Are you good at spotting spies, sir?'

My toes turned to scrunch mode as I hoped that Harry would not break the golden rule never to joke with customs officers, anywhere, at any time. But having landed in one piece he was in rollicking good form. He promptly looked around the customs area.

'I'll show you how good I am. For instance – see that man over there, looking as if butter wouldn't melt in his mouth?'

He got no further – within seconds he was paddling the air as he was marched off to a security room while I followed, mouthing words like 'he was only joking', 'really – just a silly bet'.

Harry looked as if he was about to pass out as a security man – at least, that is what I thought he must be – emptied the contents of his suitcases all over the customs officer's desk.

'Sir,' I said, pulling myself up to my best height, which unfortunately is not exactly tall. 'Please understand, what my friend, my writing partner here, means is that he was given that badge as a *joke*. It is a prize for spying on *theatrical* agents. He is an actor, a comedy actor, sir. That is a joke award that actors give each other when they have spied more theatrical agents than anyone else has. As I say – he is a *comedy* actor.'

Harry gave me a dark look because of course he did straight parts too. 'I can show you my Equity card,' he said, regaining his colour slightly.

The security man started to laugh.

'You English! Of course. You're a comedy actor. I just noticed it on your passport. I love actors. I have a cousin who's an actor. He waits tables too, but mostly he acts when he's not waiting tables.'

He looked at me. 'And you're a writer?'

'We write together.'

'But you're not married?'

'Partners – we are in a writing partnership,' I explained.

'Well, it's been a pleasure.' He looked at Melville's badge again. 'But if you don't mind, I think we'll confiscate this. Don't want any more misunderstandings. Your badge, sir, will make a great exhibit in our exhibition next year. You wouldn't believe the things we've confiscated – rubber ladies, shrunken heads from the South Seas, and now your badge. Won't that be something? I hope you'll feel proud.'

Harry gave his badge a sad parting look after which we were whisked away to our New York hotel. Stuart – our new friend the winking man – was now in charge of us.

'Well, that was a close-run thing—'

'Nearest-run, Lottie. That is the quotation. "The nearest-run thing you ever saw in your life" – spoken by the Duke of Wellington after the Battle of Waterloo. And by the way, since we're on the subject, I am not just a comedy actor.'

'I know, I am sorry about that, but we were in a bit of a jam.'

I left Harry while I went to my own room and stared out of the window at the beautiful sight of Central

Park below. It was beginning to snow, and somehow that made it even lovelier. Soon we would be boarding a train for Los Angeles, but before that happened I wanted to walk down Fifth Avenue in the snow, which I did, leaving Harry sleeping off his dreadful experience with the security man thinking he only did comedy.

The next morning Stuart called for us. His expression was funereal.

'Mr Zuckerman's plans have changed,' he announced. 'You are to stay here in New York for the next few days. It means we have to change your train tickets to Los Angeles – something to do with him seeing a kinescope of the last show. He had to fly out there to explain certain things. He's coming back soon, and you will of course have to be on hand.'

'Does he need any jokes yet?'

'Oh, he always needs jokes,' Stuart answered. 'And by the way, everyone calls me Stu, except for my mother, and what she calls me, happily, is unrepeatable. Where can I take you in New York?'

Harry chose the Empire State Building, which surprised me because he doesn't like heights. He had explained, more than once, that if he climbed up them he had an uncontrollable urge to throw himself off. On occasion I had to hold the back of his jacket when he was in the front row of the dress circle.

I soon realised why he chose the Empire State Building.

'What are you trying to see exactly, Harry, what is it you are exactly trying to see?' I demanded as Stu held him firmly by the jacket.

'Home,' he said, swallowing hard. 'I'm trying to see the Earls Court Road, and Dermot.'

'Not Dermot, Harry. Definitely not Dermot.'

'Who is this Dermot?' Stu wanted to know.

'His flatmate,' I said, briefly.

'Are they such close friends?'

'No, Harry can't stand him. He just wants to see if Dermot's pinching his butter.'

Stu took me aside while Harry continued to stare out. 'He's your writing partner, right?'

'That's quite enough.'

'He's a bit eccentric, yes?'

I considered this. 'No, not eccentric – mad.'

'He's probably a genius and it weighs heavily on him.'

'Well, that is a possibility, but just at the moment I think we should all go back to the hotel and have something nice to eat and drink.'

Which was what we did, little knowing that it was the start of endless episodes of 'let's go and have something nice' because nothing at all was happening. We kept asking Stu for news from Mr Zuckerman, but his answers were always in the evasive.

Harry started to panic.

'He's got our passports, Lottie, and our smallpox certificates. Supposing we never get them back? We might never see Dingley Dell or Earls Court again.'

'I know, we'll have to stay in New York for the rest of our lives,' I said happily.

For me that was a rather marvellous thought but not for Harry, who immediately demanded to go back up the Empire State Building to try and see the Earls Court Road.

At last there was news.

'Mr Zuckerman will not be taking you to Hollywood, or rather Los Angeles, at the moment. He'd rather you stay here and become part of ... that is, write for *The Gerry Andrews Show*. He thinks your line on things will suit Gerry just fine. You will be moving from here,' Stu went on, glancing round the sumptuous suite.

'Going home?'

'No, no, we can't let you talented guys go! No, the studio has a very cosy apartment that will be quite adequate for your needs.'

Once again the apartment had a fine view of the Park, but it was so cosy that two people could not stand together in the kitchen. The sitting room was a touch-knees affair.

'Just as well we get on, Aitch,' I said tersely, because I had just inspected the kitchen cupboards and found only glasses, which said quite a lot about the previous writers to have occupied the flat.

The hall porter directed us to Lewis & Conger and we bought some china to eat off.

'Our writers eat out,' Stu told me when he called by to find me unwrapping the plates and cups. 'Or else they use their fingers.'

What now lay ahead of us was writing jokes for Gerry Andrews, so we bought every newspaper that was printed every day, watched the news on television, and wrote a sheaf of American one-liners.

'They'll never use them,' Harry said happily. 'We'll get the sack sure as eggs are chickens.'

We didn't go to rehearsals but Stu invited us to watch the latest kinescope, which was only viewed after the show had gone out.

'What a crazy system,' Harry told him. 'Why not view it before the show goes out and then you can do something about it?'

'That's just the way we do things over here.'

The evening our particular show went out to a live audience of untold millions we sat with our fellow scribblers. No one introduced themselves. There were only tense smiles, and then the show began.

We were hardly five minutes in when the man next to Harry got up and left.

'Is he unwell?' Harry whispered to his neighbour.

'He's sick as a dog. His gag just went flat. That's him done.' The writer pulled a finger across his throat. 'Gerry doesn't forgive. That poor guy will be taking the subway home, if he can afford it.'

This cheered Harry up so much he simply could not take the smile off his face and I could see he was crossing his fingers that none of our jokes would get even a titter. To his horror and my amazement they all got woofers.

'You sure can write American,' Stu told us as he showed us to the lift. Harry couldn't understand it.

'They've got all these guys over here who've been brought up with gags and one-liners and they use us? I mean this is the land of great comedy.'

He was almost indignant.

'Maybe they're all out in Hollywood, or maybe they've all had to do National Service or whatever they do here and haven't got back yet?'

The thing about *The Gerry Andrews Show* was that by British standards it was not very long. What with the sponsors insisting on breaks what seemed like every five seconds plus time for the other acts, there really wasn't very much material needed.

We went on writing jokes for the show for the next few weeks until it ended its run, by which point even I was ready to go home if only to sample Mrs Graham's roast beef once more.

But it seemed that Mr Zuckerman had other plans for us.

'Mr Zuckerman thinks you will be most useful to him for his new shows,' Stu announced.

'We don't think we can stay for more shows,' we both said at once.

Stu gave us a firm and steady look, not a wink in sight. I knew what that meant. It meant that he had our passports and without them we could not leave the US of A.

'You won't need passports to go to Hollywood, Harry, and they'll let you on the train without going through customs,' he joked. 'They're in safekeeping, believe me. The studio has them. You'll meet up with some new people in Los Angeles.'

I took Stu aside.

'Why do you need our passports?'

'In case we need to lock you up—'

'For writing bad jokes?'

'That's the least of it.'

I must have looked alarmed.

'Don't worry, Lottie. You'll like Hollywood. You'll like the train journey, and the weather. You'll definitely like the weather. You leave from Grand Central tomorrow.'

Harry revelled in the idea of taking a train. He had seen so many movies featuring them he knew it would be great. Smiling attendants, glamorous passengers, wonderful food ... it would be everything he liked.

I was sad to leave New York and our touch-knees sitting room, and seeing shows, and eating at Sardi's and all that, but Harry was already whistling songs from great train journey musicals, or at least I think that's what they were.

Harry packed for both of us because having done tatty theatrical tours he was very good at it. He was also very good at ironing, for the same reason.

'We won't last long in Hollywood, Lottie. You'll see,' he said as we settled ourselves into our train seats. 'One look at our material and they'll send us packing. I don't know how we lasted on *The Gerry Andrews Show*.'

It took three days to get to Hollywood, days during which we played Scrabble and wrote jokes we knew were probably going to be far too clever for television audiences.

'They won't want any wit, satire or irony, Lottie-bags,' Harry said happily.

Occasionally he stuck his head out of the train window and shouted at some luckless country person standing by the track, waving his hat at the train: 'Do you understand irony?'

Remembering Stu's words about us getting locked up, I finally stopped him. 'You don't want to get arrested for insulting American citizens. Now that would be ironic. Or maybe just funny.'

We were met at the train station by a studio car and whisked off to our hotel. The grandest in Hollywood bar none, entirely due to Harry's reluctance to get on an aeroplane, which was not just ironic – but hilarious.

I was so thankful to have arrived I fell asleep, only to be woken by Harry. 'We're wanted,' he said briefly.

Mr Zuckerman had sent someone for us. 'Hallo, I'm Stu,' he said.

Stu-two was a great character; to say that he was a live wire would be to under-describe him. Harry was used to working with all sorts of characters, but Stu-two was a box of fireworks – just saying 'hi' to him was a match to set off his ceaseless display of rockets, whizz-bangs and meteors.

'Vitamin C, guys?' he asked once he had stopped talking for a few seconds. He took some tablets out of his top pocket, putting them in Harry's. 'You're sure going to need extra vitamins when you start working on *The Mary Day Show*. Best to learn her signature tune – but perhaps you know it already?' 'Course you do – just follow me.' He started to sing in a commendably tuneful voice: *'Day of Days, this is my Day of Days*. Come on! Sing, sing, sing – you'll get both barrels if you don't know her sig tune, preferably saluting while singing it, folks. Follow me, please.'

As we started to follow him round our suite, saluting and singing, my thoughts ran back to my room in Dingley Dell and our space at Harry's flat, with the writing screen to protect us from Dermot. How far had we come to be reduced to this? The answer, of course, was very far indeed. We were in Hollywood: room service, producers, Stuarts both one and two at our beck and call.

'Okay, follow me until we enter the witch's cave, whereupon you will be abandoned by your guardian angel – that's me. Nothing can save you from the big She Wolf.'

We followed him, silently wishing we were back in Earls Court with the traffic roaring past the windows. For once in his life not even Harry had anything to say. The production office was downtown from our hotel, but we walked to it still singing 'Day of Days' with Harry improvising, which he did very well.

Once at the office we were shown up to a white-painted room with a desk and two chairs. In the middle of the desk lay what was quite obviously a script.

'Is this our homework?' Harry joked.

Stu-two nodded and he gave him a 'good luck with that' look before shutting the door and leaving us.

'You read it, out loud, and I'll try and laugh,' I said nervously, because the expression on Stu-two's face did not bode well.

Harry read scripts very well – not all actors do, actually, don't get me started about how some actors read. And I don't just mean Dermot.

Harry finished reading and looked across the desk at me. 'LOTTIE!'

'What?' I asked, raising my head.

'You're alive then?'

'I daresay I am,' I admitted. 'But really, what a thing! That is not a comedy script, it is a trip down boring lane, a colossal exercise in boredom. It's so banal. I mean this woman does nothing except make jelly.'

'They are sponsored by a jelly and cream manufacturers.'

I covered my ears because Harry was shouting.

'We can't work on this,' he said happily, lowering his voice. 'We'll have to go home, Lottie-bags.'

For once I was in complete agreement, but before I could say anything the door opened and it was Stu-two again.

'Sick bowl needed?' he asked, gleefully dancing into the room. 'Shall I ring for the studio doc?'

I stood up because I wanted to make my point clear.

'We can't be of any use to this.' I pointed to the script. 'It is dead. We are in absolute agreement on this. We pronounce it dead on arrival.'

Harry nodded, all the while flicking through the pages and shaking his head.

'She's right. Nothing to be done. Not even oxygen will revive this dross. Talk about a kitchen pinafore script! That's what we call them in England – kitchen pinny scripts.'

Stu-two looked delighted and put a Vitamin C tablet under his tongue, which made his mouth foam.

'Follow me to the witch's cave.' He stopped suddenly and lowered his voice. 'Don't faint on me but she looks like a slug in a wig at this time of the morning.' He rolled his eyes. 'Actually, that's not fair on slugs.'

He was not wrong. Mary Day was sitting at a desk surrounded by what I knew must be downtrodden miserable writers. They barely glanced up as we came in. She, on the other hand, stared at us as she slowly took some plastic rollers out of her hair.

'Here are the British writers, Miss Day,' Stu-two said, indicating us.

'Well, I didn't think they were chorus girls, Stuart,' she said, intent on lighting a cigarette. 'Sit down,' she nodded at one chair.

Harry sat down and I promptly sat on his knee.

The writers all started to laugh as Stu-two brought me a chair of my own.

'So you two work together. Rows every hour of the day, I guess?'

Harry always got affronted when someone said that, which they quite frequently did, so it was tiring for him.

I looked at the ceiling and wondered if there wasn't something else for people to say when it came to one man and one woman working together.

'I couldn't work with my husband,' Miss Day said, turning round to address her captive audience. 'I would murder him.'

None of the writers smiled.

'So what do you think of the script we left you to read?'

Harry looked at the other writers, knowing that at least one of them must have been involved.

'I never criticise another writer's work in front of them,' he said pointedly.

'Okay, guys, leave. Not you, Stuart, you can stay. We all know you can't write your own name.'

'Charming, isn't she?' Stu-two whispered to me as the other writers trouped out of the room.

'So, Mr British Writer, what do you have to say about this script?'

'Do you want the truth?

'Of course.'

'It's melted jelly. And sour cream too.'

At this Stu-two turned away, clapping his hand to his mouth, or maybe he had put another tablet in it.

'It's what we call in England a kitchen pinafore comedy, which is okay if it's funny, but this isn't funny.'

'So what are you going to do about it?'

'Go back to England.'

'Are you that yellow?'

'Yes, oh, yes.' Harry smiled happily at the astonished Mary Day, and I felt so happy for him I could almost have helped the wretched woman take the rest of her rollers out – I say almost because although I knew sacrifices had to be made at all times, I might have passed on the chance at the last minute.

'Whatever they need to make them stay, give it to them,' Mary Day commanded, turning to Stu-two. 'Anything and everything they want – just get a script out of them.' She suddenly started to laugh. 'Kitchen pinafore indeed!'

Her laughter followed us past the writers waiting outside, and into the lift.

'Isn't she something else?' Stu-two asked, without a trace of fondness.

Harry looked ahead of him, thinking. He knew we were on a sticky wicket. Write a fresh script for the beastly woman and we just might get our passports back – oh, and our smallpox certificates. Don't write the script and we would have to do something drastic. The studio could 'lose' our documents and that would mean endless waiting, and new passports, and heaven only knew what colour tape.

'Okay, Lottie-bags, pens out – ideas please!'

To say that writing for that woman was a slog was to say the least.

'We have to slug it out, Lottie. After that, with any luck, we can make a break for it.'

The show we wrote was in the *I Love Lucy* mode. There was not much else you could do with two sets, a kettle and a few changes of apron. The husband was a useless idiot – obviously based on the Slug's own choice – and he actually caused us the most trouble until we hit on the idea of making him a gardener.

His declared war on slugs gave us such undercover fun that somehow our gaiety must have translated itself to the script because the Slug herself adored it.

'Please not more weeks holed up here—'

'I know. It's terrible, Harry. Room service, a television, a radio, a fridge filled with every drink imaginable. It is a living hell, I do see that.'

'You know what I mean.'

'I do. Movie stars everywhere, cocktails in the evening. I think a letter to *The Times* is needed.'

'The movie stars don't even speak to us.'

'Film people don't talk to television people, you know that. They think television has killed film. Besides, they live in fear of all their old films being re-run, which will show up their ages.'

Despite Harry's moans we were engaged in writing another script. The gardening husband had caught fire with the other writers. Stu-two brought us information from the front line. We started to wonder if he could be trusted. He seemed to know too much about what we were writing. Whenever he came into the suite we hid our work, and when he left we turned out the pencil vases, which he continually filled and re-filled – to such an extent that we suspected he was putting recording devices in them.

Remembering that we were also meant to be working for MI5 in a strong and silent way, of an evening we would sit straining to hear other people's conversations in the cocktail lounge. One evening we must have seemed rather too interested because a very handsome couple followed us into the lift.

After a few exchanges of looks between themselves the male partner asked us in a very attractive voice, 'Tell me, do you party?'

'Oh, yes,' Harry answered blithely. 'We party all the time. We love parties. Wine and cheese – all sorts.'

They started to laugh.

'We're on this number, here's our card – call us, do.'

I frowned. I didn't like the way they were looking at us as if we were ripe fruit. Back in our suite I put their card on my desk. The following evening our hotel telephone rang. It was the unmistakable voice of the man in the lift.

'Come on over,' he said. 'Come on over and we'll party.'

'I'll call you back,' I said.

Harry thought we should go in the interests of international relations. I thought I had quite enough relations already, but I did see his point.

From the moment we went into their suite, which was on low lights with accompanying low music – Frank Sinatra's *Songs for Swinging Lovers* – I felt as if I should have a small lady's gun, white and silver if possible, in my handbag.

I quickly thought of Commander Steerforth and Arabella and all the wonderful people I worked with when I wasn't on sabbatical in Hollywood.

What would they do in this situation? They would act calmly – that would be Arabella – and correctly – that would be Commander Steerforth.

'I wonder if you could turn up the music? I am slightly deaf,' I said. 'And the lighting. My writing partner here, Harry, is short-sighted.'

They did so, but only fractionally, as they handed us glasses of champagne.

'*Don't drink – it's drugged!*' I found myself silently screaming to Harry, while at the same time I did see that he too was alert to danger because he was scratching his left ear, which I knew he always did in rehearsal when he wanted to signal to fellow actors about the director '*we've got a right one here*'.

For the next few minutes we kept raising our glasses to God Bless America, and Here's to the Queen of

England, and Long Live Hollywood, and goodness knows what other toasts, while our lips took only token sips at our glasses.

'We thought we would take room service – in there.'

The relevant door was open. We could see that 'in there' was a bedroom with a vast bed.

'Why not come to our suite? Our room service is faster and our "in there" much bigger,' Harry said, putting on his most droll expression.

For some reason they seemed to think this was not just amusing but hilarious. Before they could finish laughing we put down our glasses and fled to our suite, calling to them to follow 'in five minutes'.

I caught Harry by the arm as he ran past me into the suite, slamming the door behind me.

'She's a Ruski!' I said.

'Do stop speaking Bulldog Drummond lingo, Lottie,' Harry implored even as he emptied out the pencil vases, which was actually his nightly routine.

'No, she is, I spotted it at once. They never say "the". Russians always say "bedroom", not "the bedroom". Didn't you notice?'

'Her accent is impeccable – pure Long Island. And as for the bed, it didn't need a "the" in front of it as far as I was concerned.'

I picked up their card from my desk. 'I tell you, she is a Ruski.'

Whether I was right or not, we took the telephone off the hook and ignored the plaintive little knocks at the door of our suite, turning up the television and living off what was in our fridge.

Curiosity as well as our duty to MI5 took us back to the cocktail lounge the next evening.

The moment the couple saw us they came over to where we were sitting. We valiantly pinned on our most polite expressions.

'You hurt our feelings,' they told us. 'We were sincere in our invitation. We thought you were nice people.'

'I'm afraid you got that wrong,' I said firmly. 'We're both writers. Writers are not nice people.'

They went back to their usual places, looking digni-fied and hurt.

'You shouldn't have given their names to you know who last night,' Harry said. 'Poor things, look at them, we've broken their hearts.'

'There's something about them,' I said, going all Arabella and mysterious on him.

'Never mind that, we have a script to finish.'

Which we did indeed have, and did indeed do. We finished it just before the first we had written was printed up and sent to our suite courtesy of Stu-two.

Harry immediately seized on it and took it to read in his bedroom while I watched television with my mouth open, which had become a bit of an unfortunate habit with me when watching American telly.

'LOTTIE!'

Harry threw open the door. He took a deep breath. He had a very good diaphragm so was good at doing deep breaths.

'There is not one word of this which is ours. NOT ONE WORD. No – I tell a lie. There is one line left, which is mine – no, it's yours – no, it's both of ours. Just one line, I tell you. It's outrageous. I'm going to put in a call to Dewi.'

'Dewi will be asleep, Harry.'

Dewi had nothing to say from his bed, which was good because Harry was already packing our bags. In the middle of his suitcase-filling, Stu-two dropped by.

'You can hire anyone, why hire us?' Harry asked.

Stu-two tried to look surprised that Harry was so upset.

'That's television,' he said, sighing. 'I mean Tuesday is rewrite day, we have to keep other writers happy, and rewriting television is not exactly the movies. But listen, don't go – you two deliver great material. We appreciate it, really we do. Unpack and stay for one more script. Make the Slug happy, huh?'

'Just one then.'

Stu-two put a Vitamin C tablet in his mouth and chewed for a minute. 'Here's a thing – quite a thing. A couple along the way from here ... guess what?'

At this I stopped filling the pencil vases for him, and even Harry stopped fuming for a second.

'They've been arrested for being over-sexed?' he quipped.

'Not even close. They've been arrested – yes, for being Russian spies. How about that? The Slug wants to put them in a script for the show. She wants Mary Day to arrest them in the supermarket. Knock them out with her kettle and tie them up with her apron. And I wish I was kidding but I'm not.'

It was my turn to breathe in and out fast.

'Well, I never,' Harry said, and I could see that he wished he had Melville's badge back.

After Stu-two left I didn't say 'see' to Harry. I didn't say 'I told you so'. I just said: 'The.'

The fact 'the' is a word that comes up rather a lot when you are writing did not improve our artistic relationship.

'Do you think they knew about your father?'

'Ruskis always use sex,' I said avoiding that one.

'What a thing,' Harry said, frowning. 'All a bit real, don't you think, Lottie-bags?'

The arrests were all over the newspapers and the news, which we found a bit close to home, but at least it stopped Harry from feeling bad about hurting the handsome couple's feelings. He was very sensitive like that.

After much excitement and our writing two more shows for the Slug, even Stu-two was happy to say good-bye to us.

He was very gracious, although still foaming. He gave us back our passports. Oh, and our smallpox certificates.

'You've been a terrific help. Two very talented people. The show has benefited from your scripts big time.'

I was sad to say goodbye to Los Angeles: to the clock that chimed the hour outside the window, to the gaiety of the shops, to the hotel staff who were incredibly gracious, and the barman who even put up with Harry lecturing him about how to make a proper Martini.

When we got back to Dingley Dell and Earls Court we found it was great to be home, but to be truthful Hollywood had spoiled us. I didn't realise just how much until I found myself constantly picking up the telephone to order food to be sent up. Somehow Dermot's stuffed cabbage was not quite the same.

As for Harry, he felt only too happy to be back. Arriving for work of an evening, I would find him standing on the pavement outside the flat on his way to his favourite shops – past all the slow-moving traffic – happily singing 'Day of Days'. His version.

TINY TIMES

It was Sunday at Dingley Dell. The sun was shining. Melville was playing the piano and Hal was booming at my mother. My father was mixing drinks and humming along to Melville's playing.

Downstairs Mrs Graham was cooking lunch, and Harry and I had just won an award for an episode of *The Mary Day Show* we'd entered in a writers' competition for a joke.

Needless to say, it involved Mary arresting spies in the supermarket, although Harry drew the line at her tying them up with her apron.

'Irony can go no further,' he said happily when we picked up the award from Dewi's office.

On hearing the good news Dewi immediately put our fees up, which meant that one day we might be able to buy a house and get married.

In Knightsbridge Monty was in seventh heaven, laying out a delicious buffet for Arabella and Zuzu, who was back in town. All Mademoiselle's favourite food had been prepared. Rollo was spotless and shining, waiting to take them all round the Park in stately fashion.

Recently I'd written the start to something along the lines of a novel. As Harry only read thrillers, and Arabella still had her head in Egyptian tombs, I gave a chunk of it to Monty to read. He approved of it – with only one stipulation.

'Don't you go giving it some dreadful modern dreary ending,' he warned. 'I won't have it, really I won't. You make sure it has a Tiny Times ending.'

Tiny Times was Monty's way of saying Happy Days – always said with a contented sigh, naturally.

It came from Tiny Tim in *A Christmas Carol* famously saying at the end of the book, 'God bless us, every one!'

I lived in dread of offending Monty, as well I might, so I was going to end my book with Tiny Times, and Harry and I dancing down the street back to his flat where we'd placed our award on a shelf so we could see it. If we got stuck at work we sang a snatch of 'Day of Days' and that always did the trick. It also annoyed Dermot, which was good.

Tiny Times indeed.

TV AND FILM WITH TERENCE BRADY

Comedy

No, Honestly Series
Yes, Honestly Series
Pig in the Middle Series
Father Matthew's Daughter Series
Oh Madeline Series
Play for Today Series: 'Making the Play'

Drama

Take Three Girls Series
Upstairs, Downstairs Series
Thomas and Sarah Series
Nanny Series
Forever Green Series

Films

Magic Moments
Love with a Perfect Stranger

Stage Plays

The Shell Seekers
I Wish I Wish

A NOTE ON THE AUTHOR

Charlotte Bingham wrote her first book, *Coronet Among the Weeds*, a memoir of her life as a debutante, at the age of 19. It was published in 1963 and became an instant bestseller. Her father, John Bingham, the 7th Baron Clanmorris, was a member of MI15 where Charlotte Bingham worked as a secretary. He was an inspiration for John le Carré's character George Smiley.

Charlotte Bingham went on to write thirty-three internationally bestselling novels and the memoir *MI5 and Me*. In partnership with her late husband Terence Brady, she wrote a number of successful plays, films and TV series including *Upstairs Downstairs* and *Take Three Girls*. She lives in Somerset.

charlottebingham.com